Keeper of the Keys
A Warden's Notebook

by
Wayne K. Patterson
Betty L. Alt

Published by
My Friend, The Printer, Inc.

Printed by My Friend, The Printer, Inc.
410 West Fifth Street
Pueblo, Colorado 81003

Cover Design and Layout by Diane Hochevar and Naomi Milavec

International Standard Book Number: 0-9715847-5-3 $18.95

DEDICATION

Dedicated to my son Monte, who, as a Denver police officer, spent 25 years recruiting denizens for the prison, and to my wife Mary and daughter Tammy, who lived with me on prison grounds

and

to my longtime friend and "pardner," James P. O'Neil, who was assisting in compiling this book when he went to his eternal rest

and

to all the correctional and law enforcement workers I have met during my career, whose dedication, strength, courage and support have been an inspiration to me over the years.

INTRODUCTION

During my career in corrections, I have often found myself searching for a scrap of paper on which to scribble a note to remind me of a happening – an act of violence or of kindness, an act of humor and fun, a spoken word, a small victory won, a human fault exposed or an act of bravery that I felt must be recorded in some way. If I were successful in capturing the happening, I would later expand it into a short story and put it in a notebook which I kept near my desk. These stories are all based on facts, but some names have been changed to protect innocent persons and persons who have changed their lives.

My co-author Betty Alt has enabled the scribbles in a tattered notebook or my verbal musings to become real people – officers who went to work daily in one of the most hazardous occupations in our society, wardens and other professionals in the criminal justice system, and confined men and women who had lost their freedom, but still retained their distinct personalities.

These tales and my verbal reflections reflect a much different era of correctional services. The reader must remember that prisons are mirrors of society and, therefore, these stories reflect society's view of prisoners in an earlier period of history. The warden was much more autocratic. (A grand jury once referred to me as an *emperor*, a "one man" operation.) He was responsible to the governor through an appointed director of all institutions, and a warden's primary duties were prescribed in the state statutes.

Punishment of rebellious prisoners was much more harsh.* Whipping, long periods of isolation and severe diet restrictions were standard procedures until they were banned by the executive order of Governor Dan Thornton and orders of the federal courts in early 1950.

This book represents a cross section of prison life as it was lived during the turbulent 1960s and early 1970s. It is an abstract of my thirty years of "hands on" experience in the administration of the Men's Reformatory at Buena Vista and the Colorado State Penitentiary, and as Director of Corrections and Chief Executive Officer of the Denver Sheriff's Department, Executive Director of the Department of Parole for Colorado, and Chairman of the Parole Board.

For those readers unfamiliar with prison terminology, a short glossary has been included in the Appendix. Unless otherwise noted, photos used were given to me or accumulated by me over my career. Many of these have been duplicated and placed in the Local History Section of the Cañon City Public Library, the Museum of Colorado Prisons at Cañon City or the Western History Section of the Denver Public Library.

The authors would like to thank the following: Pat Kant, Administrator of the Museum of Colorado Prisons and her staff for help in researching factual details for the book; Cara Fisher, Director of the Local History Section of the Cañon City Library for the recovery of photos relating to the stories; Col. (Ret.) Bill Alt for his constructive advice during the writing and the many friends and colleagues who encouraged the authors during the planning and writing of the book.

– Wayne K. Patterson

---

* See Appendix for disciplinary procedures.

TABLE OF CONTENTS

Men
Behind Bars

A TRIP TO
THE PRISON BARBER SHOP

You just never got caught!
- Roy Best

On the first of each month, as Executive Director of Parole, I would visit each institution and interview the prisoners who were to appear at the parole board that month. In April 1952 I happened to be at the penitentiary* and decided that I needed a haircut, so I went to the prison officers' barber shop in the central building

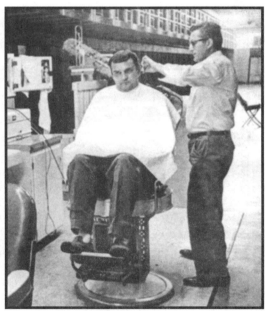

Photo courtesy of George Crouter.

where I ran into Warden Roy Best. He was also having some tonsorial services, and we visited a bit until I was summoned to a

---

* The Colorado State Penitentiary was the only prison at that time.

chair. My barber (one of the convicts as all barbers in the institution were convicts) had just started to put an apron on me when, to my surprise, he said, "Mr. Patterson, do you remember me?"

I turned and looked at him and replied, "Yes. You are Jeff of the 'Mutt and Jeff' stickups." He and his partner, Kurtis, had been tabbed as the "Mutt and Jeff Bandits" by the Denver police detectives due to their respective heights.[*]

Chuckling, the barber said, "I mean do you recognize me from years ago when we were going to grade school? I'm Fred Walcott."

I looked again and recognized him from the old westside Denver neighborhood. We were friends through the seventh and eighth grades in Baker Junior High and visited each other's homes as we lived across the alley from each other. His family were nice, middle-class folks, and his mother always produced cookies and milk for us after we and the other kids played football in the streets. Both of our families would have been considered poor but always had food to share. I had not seen nor heard of Fred in more than twenty years.

Finally, I said, "Well, Freddie, how in hell did you get here?"

"So my family could have a nice Thanksgiving dinner, I stole a turkey that was hanging in the windows of the butcher shop on South Broadway," he related, "and to shorten the story, I got sent to the boy's Industrial School at Golden."

Fred tugged one corner of the apron over my coat collar to make sure no hair would fall down my neck and continued: "While I was at the industrial school my mother died and my father and younger brother moved back to Kansas and left no address

---

[*] The partner was about 6' 2" and the barber was about 5' 6". Mutt and Jeff were cartoon characters in many U.S. newspapers well into the mid fifties – one character extremely tall and the other very short.

for me. I stayed a few days at a mission on Larimer Street and committed a few burglaries. I got caught and spent the next year in 'Bueny.' (See Glossary.) When I got out, I was lost. I met Kurtis and we started a long string of stickups. The police and papers called us the 'Mutt and Jeff Bandits.' We liked the label and continued until we made a mistake."

Stopping for a few seconds as if to ponder his earlier days, Fred grinned and followed on with his explanation. "The Deputy Chief of the State Patrol,[*] in plain clothes, was getting into an unmarked car when Kurt and I were running from a stickup of a drugstore in east Denver. I put my gun on him and tried to take his car, but you know how big he is. He hit me and so I kept running." Again, Fred stopped speaking and gave a small sigh. "That run-in with the deputy turned into a twenty-year hitch. We might have got less, but the 'Dep' was mad and came to court and testified against us."

During the time of the storytelling, silence had settled over the shop. Warden Best was still in the chair, and the shoe shine man who usually sang, danced and played a mouth harp had been completely quiet. I finally broke the silence and spoke to Warden Best. "Warden, you're an old hand at this business, and you've heard the story. This man and I came from nearly the same background. He spent his early years on a farm in Kansas and I on a ranch near Montrose. Both families went broke and moved to the old west side of Denver. We had the same education, lived through a harsh Depression." I cited several more things we had in common for comparison and then added, "Now he winds up doing twenty years, and I wind up as Parole Director. What do you think is the reason?"

Best, always the joker, looked at me and said, "That's easy, you bastard. You just never got caught!"

---

[*] Fred was referring to Gilbert Carrel who later became Chief of the Patrol.

He got the response he wanted. All of the convicts in the barbershop howled with laughter.

Off and on for the next ten years, Fred cut my hair and we always had a few memories to recall of the old Denver "west side." He was always good-humored, and he eventually served his sentence and was paroled to California. I lost track of him after he completed his parole and never heard of him again.

THE BALLAD OF
"ELS" AND "DICK"

The very prison walls began to reel.
                                    - Oscar Wilde

Ellsworth was a big handsome man, six feet tall and weighing over 200 pounds. "Els" (as he was called by most) had wavy blonde hair and an envious reputation as a ladies' man. While hitchhiking from his home in Wisconsin to visit a cousin in Reno who had promised him employment, he was given a ride by a salesman named Gray near Akron, Colorado. Before they traveled far, Els murdered the salesman and left his body in a barn on a ranch in northeastern Colorado. Shortly thereafter Els was apprehended near Salida, convicted of the murder and sentenced to life in prison. (Life sentences were "for life" unless clemency was exercised by the Governor.)

Els spent the next ten years in prison and, while appealing his case to the courts, educated himself as a medical and dental assistant. He was given his own room in the hospital and wore a white uniform instead of the regulation uniform. Since he was trusted, his presence any place in the institution was never questioned.

During his imprisonment, his cousin in Reno, who was married and had a small daughter, continued to keep in touch. The cousin's wife, Beryl, and the daughter were on a trip to visit relatives in Chicago, and the cousin asked Beryl to stop in Colorado and visit Els. (Roy Best, who was warden at that time, told me later "that big good looking bastard dressed in white and behind bars charmed and hypnotized her.") In any event, Beryl continued to visit, finally divorced the cousin and moved to Cañon City to be closer to Els.

Best was eventually suspended as warden, and for two years thereafter Harry Tinsley was designated acting warden. After much pleading from Els and Beryl, Tinsley authorized the marriage of the couple.* The marriage was not consummated, but the ceremony was held in the warden's office and the vows duly taken. Lots of "well wishers" were on hand to participate in the union of a man doing life in prison and his cousin's ex-wife.

Life in prison continued as usual, but Els seemed to have found a prescription for hope. His marriage had yielded some romantic publicity which stressed that he had a loving wife and daughter. It was thought that, possibly, Governor Dan Thornton** might consider an application for clemency.

At that time I was Executive Director of the State Department of Parole and had appointed a parole agent named Richard ("Dick") who appeared sympathetic to Els' present station in life. His new friend "Dick" had discussed a possible appeal to Dick's close friend "Governor Dan." For Els, everything was shining as if through rose-colored glasses.

However, time slowly dragged on and events became more complicated. Friend "Dick's" promises were not happening, long talks with his friend were not productive, and without consummation the marriage was beginning to erode. The story of Els then unfolded in the following manner:

---

* The rule in those days was that no prisoner could be married without the Warden's consent.

** Dan Thornton was Chairman of the Parole Board, and Lt. Governor Gordon Allott was the Vice Chairman.

I was on a regular trip from my Denver office and went in to the prison at 8:30 a.m. on June 8, 1953. Heading to the Deputy Warden's office to talk to Captain Gentry, I was waylaid by Els. He was obviously very upset and agitated and said that he must see me at ONCE. I told him to come to the parole office and I would talk with him right then. He was nearly purple in the face and told me that he had lost everything and planned to kill Dick when he returned to the institution. Dick was on an errand downtown at the time and, since I considered the threat serious, I called the front entrance and told the officer there not to let Dick back into the prison when he returned.

Then I told Els to "settle down and give me the story." This he did – seven and a half typed pages on flimsy orange-colored paper, dated May 8, 1953. Briefly, the account detailed his marriage to Beryl, his growing friendship with Parole Consultant Dick, his purchasing an auto from Dick for Beryl, his learning that Beryl was pregnant and Dick offering to try and obtain an abortion for Beryl and, finally, his awareness that Beryl and his "friend" Dick had been having an affair, financed in great part by Els.

After reading the account and talking at length with the cuckold, I went to the front gate and told Dick that he was suspended and ordered him to be in the Denver office the following Monday morning. Then I went to Acting Warden Tinsley's office and gave him El's epistle. A little later the warden and I went to find Beryl who confirmed the tale, with some additional embellishments. Tinsley was shocked, and I think he could see some future adverse publicity if the story became public knowledge. After all, it was just a little over a year since the wedding, and this was still fresh in the public's mind.*

---

* The story was leaked by someone; however, there was a great deal of confusion, and so no newspaper article ever appeared. One legislator asked me if the perpetrator was a Parole Board member.

The following Monday I sent Dick in search of other employment! Els would serve another twelve years in prison, but he and Beryl came to some sort of understanding and continued their disrupted marriage. (Dick's consummation of the nuptials apparently didn't count.)

After I was appointed Warden at the Buena Vista facility in the mid fifties, I transferred Els to that institution to serve as a medical and dental assistant, and he reinstated his appeal to the courts. In 1962 or 1963 the court ordered a new trial, and since the evidence and the witnesses had disappeared in the intervening twenty-two years, he could not be successfully prosecuted. Attorney General Duke Dunbar ordered him released.

Els obtained a job as a medical and dental supply salesman, and he and Beryl lived in Buena Vista a short period of time before his company moved him to Boston. He visited me once and corresponded a couple of times. He died in Boston in his fifties,* still married to Beryl and, apparently happy. So, the "Ballad of Els and Dick" had a happy curtain call.

---

* My information on his death was relayed by Dr. Smith, the institutional physician, who was fond of Els and kept in touch with him for several years. Smith said that Els was as good a medical technician as any with whom he had worked.

BEHAVIOR MODIFICATION
– AN EARLY EXPERIENCE

Though this be madness, yet there is method in't.
-Shakespeare: Hamlet

B ehavior modification is a phrase much heard in the field of corrections in the past several years. It comes with the question: What is being done by the corrections community to change the attitudes and subsequent behavior of those committed to its custody for anti-social activity. I had an early exposure to this process at Cañon City by one described by some as a "madman."

In the spring of 1965, perhaps because of the season and nature's stirring at that time of year, two prisoners who were gang leaders organized their followers for a "showdown" in the Big Yard.* There were approximately 75 to 100 prisoners in the two factions who armed themselves with clubs, "shanks" (home-made knives), baseball bats and miscellaneous other weapons. They improvised body armor by using football helmets with magazines, catalogs and boards stuffed beneath their shirts.

---

* The "Big Yard" was the entire northeast area of the prison and contained a regulation football field, baseball diamond, bleacher seats for games, boxing ring, cement tables, etc. There were two smaller areas in the prison designated as "little yards."

11

The sizeable disturbance started early during an afternoon recreation period. The officers in the towers on the walls responded immediately. In accordance with the rules, officers were to fire one volley over the heads of the combatants and, after a short pause, a second into the ground at their feet. Since the convicts knew that the next volley would be fired directly into the fighters' anatomy, the fight was short lived. The prisoners all "hit the ground" as the rules directed.

The incipient riot under control, twelve ring leaders (six from each faction) were individually tried before the Prison Discipline Court and given the usual thirty-six days discipline* and then confined in single cells on two separate floors in the Segregation Unit in Cell House 3. They were not to be released to the general prison population until I ordered otherwise as they were dangerous to each other and to the security of the prison. I conferred with them on a weekly basis, but they, all being "prison wise," would not promise to conform to the rules nor to refrain from any gang activity if they were returned to the general population. Except for being locked down most of the time, they were not receiving any other form of punishment. Since they did not have to work, they decided to remain in this status and test the will of the prison administration. It was a standoff that lasted several months until an unusual happening changed their collective minds regarding the benefits of modifying their attitudes and behavior.

At that time, the state mental hospital in Pueblo had no housing which could provide the proper security for its more violent residents. Such patients were transferred to the prison at Cañon City and housed in a special section of Cell House 3, where the Segregation Unit was also located. One such patient, John, was received on transfer, after the group of

---

* See Appendix for rules regarding Disciplinary Procedure.

12

twelve gang fighters had spent several months in segregation, and was confined in the opposite end of the same cell house.

John was a giant of a black man, six feet six inches in height and weighed in excess of 250 pounds. He occupied one tier of the cell house all by himself because he talked incessantly – all of the time, even in his sleep, or, maybe he never slept. Sometimes he made sense, but most of the time he made no sense at all; still, the talking was continuous, day and night. He did vary his tone of voice from loud and raucous to a monotone, but regardless of the pitch of his voice, the talk was never ending. The only relief for the officers or other prisoners in Cell House 3 was that he could not be heard in the other parts of the cell house.

In addition to his constant speech, John had several other bad habits, some of which were very unsanitary. One was particularly annoying. After eating a meal, he would defecate in his plate and toss the feces at the first officer who approached his cell. Because of this, his cell had to be cleaned daily while he showered. When John finished his shower, if he did not wish to return to his cell voluntarily, he prowled the tier naked, talking incessantly, until sufficient manpower could be gathered to wrestle him back to his abode. Due to his size and strength, it took considerable manpower to accomplish this task without injuring him.

One day, John again decided not to return to his cell after his shower. I had ordered that I was to be informed if or when this occurred, and so I went over to the Segregation Unit to observe what measures were being used to control John.* Since his cell had not yet been cleaned by the time that the number of officers necessary to handle the situation arrived on the scene, I ordered that John be placed in an empty cell away

---

* Then U. S. District Attorney Lawrence Henry had written me that he was receiving information that officers were using excessive force to control violent prisoners and suggested that I check into this matter.

from his usual area. This particular cell just happened to be on the same tier with one of the groups of six in segregation for the gang fight. John was wrestled into the cell, talking, and he continued to talk and talk and talk. Some talk even sounded threatening.

Several days later Lieutenant McDaniel, who was in charge of the Segregation Unit, came to my office with a mischievous grin on his face and said, "Warden, Toby (the leader of one of the gang factions) and the boys want to see you as soon as possible. Old John seems to have them pretty upset."

"Tell them I'll be over there tomorrow," I responded, "but make it plain that I feel that I've wasted a lot of time talking to them over the past few months, and I'm not inclined to waste any more time on them."

The next day I went to Cell House 3 and, as usual, was greeted by John who was talking fast in a very loud voice and ignoring the shouts to stop from the gang on the tier. "Warden," the gang spokesman pleaded, "you've got to get him out of here. He's been talking ever since he's been in here – day and night. He never sleeps or, if he does, he talks in his sleep. We haven't had a wink of sleep since he's been here."

"Now, boys," I said, "you know he's a mental case and can't help his talking. You'll just have to be tolerant of him."

The six prisoners joined in, all complaining at once, "You've got to get him out of here. We're going to burn him out; we can't stand it. We guarantee that we'll kill him if you don't get him out of here!"

"Well," I said, rubbing my chin, "I just don't have any other place for him right now, so he will have to stay where he is while I consider other options." When I left the tier, John was still chattering noisily as the gang members shouted threats at him.

14

Other prison problems took up my immediate attention, and I had no opportunity for a quick resolution of the problem which John had created. A day or so later, Lieutenant McDaniel came up to me in the yard with the report, "The boys on John's tier are pretty desperate as John's still going strong, talking constantly. They told me to tell you that they would like to make a deal with you."

When I arrived in the Segregation Unit shortly after lunch, all six men again tried to talk at the same time. "Get us out of here," they begged, "and we'll do anything you want. *Anything*! We'll not fight with the other gang; we'll shake hands with them. We'll go to work, take any job you give us. You'll have no more problems with us."

I said, "Men, you surely have changed since last I

Warden Patterson (second from right) with some of the gang members.

talked with you. So, I'm going to give you a couple more days, on me, to see if you're sincere and honest. I'll be over to see you again in a few days." They all howled, but they knew that I would keep my word. Two days later I ordered that they be released from segregation and reassigned to work.

However, I sensed that I had hit upon a program of "prisoner reform" that was as fulfilling to a prisoner as allowing him to escape. I told the lieutenant in Cell House 3 to assemble his "wrestling team" and move John to the floor above, to a cell on the tier adjacent to the remaining six gang members. This was done and John continued to talk and talk. A week later, the remaining six were "reformed," released from segregation and sent back to work.

As they had promised, the twelve prisoners kept their word; they all worked hard; there was no more fighting among the gangs; they obeyed the rules and would good naturedly banter with me in the yard about "the deal" we had made. They assured me that they *never* wanted to be housed with Old John again.

John was eventually taken back to the state hospital by a psychiatric group which became particularly interested in his case. Remarkably, the man, whom many considered a blithering idiot when they saw him during his stay at the prison, improved to the point that he was released from the hospital.

During the time that he was confined at the prison, I did not believe that John knew my name nor who I was. Still, during his ceaseless talking, a few comments were interpreted from his endless blather. If you listened closely, you could decipher some comments. He rambled on about Roy Best killing his father and Warden Harry Tinsley killing the rest of his family. Sometimes the words were threatening; other times they were cajoling or simply some sort of constant muttering to himself; occasionally he would burst forth with hysterical, eerie laughter. For example, if John knew that I was in the cell house, he would call out to Lt. McDaniel for me to come down to his cell so that he could talk to me. Lt. McDaniel cautioned me not to go as John had a plate full of something that he was going to throw at me when I came into sight. My better judgment, and the lieutenant's advice, caused me to call out to John that I was sorry but was in a hurry and would see him later. I never learned what was in the plate!

Several years later, to my complete surprise, I received a Christmas card from John, mailed from Fremont, Nebraska. I continued to receive cards each year for the next five or six years. The cards were signed by John but had no return address, so I was never able to acknowledge that I had received them.

However, in dealing later with recalcitrant prisoners and gangs, I often wished I could find Old John for a few days. Cruel maybe, but his being so verbally active certainly had modified the behavior of two prison gangs!

The Prison Barbershop Quartet

The prison contained a theater that could seat 1,000 inmates, and entertainment was often brought into the prison. Various organizations (such as Alcoholics Anonymous, Footprinters or some self-help groups) were invited or requested to utilize the facilities. At times, particularly close to holidays, inmates provided entertainment for their fellow prisoners or members of the above groups. Many of the entertainers were quite talented.

A STORY OF "MAMA"

If I were hanged on the highest hill,
I know whose love would follow me still, my mother.
                                    -Kipling

One summer morning about ten o'clock, I was wading through a pile of mail and dictating some responses when Officer Masse on the front entry* called and said that there was an elderly lady who wanted to see me. "She's upset, real upset," he said. "I've tried to calm her down, but no way. She's going to see you if it takes all day."

It has always been my practice to see any relative, particularly mothers of prisoners. Even if the press of business postponed an interview, I always had the secretary set a date when I could visit with the mother. This practice was my way of keeping in touch with the families of the prisoners. However, since the woman was already at the "eye," I told the officer to send her in to see me.

When I went to usher her into my office, I could she that she was obviously very agitated, angry and vocal. I asked her to sit down and tell me the reason for her aggravation. Taking a deep breath, she literally exploded.

"Warden, my kid was cussed out by the psychologist. He

---

* This was the "eye," an electronic metal detector at the entry to the prison.

cussed him out right in front of a lot of other convicts up in the big yard. The psychologist had no reason to do this, and I want something done about him." She felt that her "kid" had done nothing to deserve this verbal assault – absolutely nothing!

After this long diatribe, I took a second look at the lady. She was a tall woman with a lined face and gray hair combed back into a bun which was held in place by a couple of celluloid-looking hair pins. A "Mother Hubbard" type of blue dress, black cotton stockings and flat, heavy work shoes covered her large frame. Calloused hands that showed years of hard work and, probably, pain clutched a large purse that swung between her knees. Her jaw jutted out, and she looked me in the eye as she declared, "I'm eighty-five and my kid is all I've got. I tried to soothe her, but she was not to be soothed. She wanted the psychologist punished and without delay. (The thought crossed my mind that it was a good thing that the psychologist wasn't there or there could have been a physical assault.)

"Did you see your son this morning?" I asked.

"Yes, sir."

"And he didn't give a reason for the 'cussing'?"

"My kid said he had missed an appointment – but he gave a reason. I had left some money for him in his account,* and he had to get to the canteen before it closed. He needed some cigarettes and candy. Since he had to stand in line at the canteen, he missed the appointment."

For the first time I asked the old mother for her "kid's" name. Behind my desk was a cabinet with the record and picture of every prisoner in the institution, and I turned to search the file. From her continual use of the words "my kid," I had it in my mind

---

* Prisoners earned small amounts of money for their work within the prison, and relatives often sent some money to them. This was kept in an "account" from which they could purchase items such as cigarettes, candy, toiletries, etc. from a "canteen."

that I would be looking for a rather young prisoner. However, the only prisoner that I could find by the name she had given me was a man fifty-eight years old with a criminal record that filled both sides of the large file card – a record of con games, burglary, bogus check scams and thievery which had resulted in trips of varying lengths to seven other prisons prior to his Colorado sentence.

"Does your son have another name, an alias?" I asked the mother.

"No, I don't think so." She looked puzzled by my question.

When I showed her the photo on the card I was holding, she immediately smiled and said, "Yes, that's him. That's my kid."

My first thought was, *Mama, this jackass of a "kid" of yours has been in seven prisons, a few dozen jails and appears to be in serious need of some sort of mental health treatment. If I were the doctor and he missed an appointment, I'd be apt to cuss him out and give him a "lost time" report.* However, I had second thoughts. Here was an old, toil-worn mother, who obviously had spent the better part of her life in loving, guarding and protecting her only son. He was a proven renegade, possibly a psychopath, but if she had ever seen his faults, she had dismissed them from her mind. I decided that a lecture by me on the wrong way to rear children would accomplish nothing and would only further distress this devoted old mother.

After we had talked a while further, I told her that I would look into the matter and if the facts warranted, I would censure the psychologist for his use of bad language. (I did not tell her that I planned to speak to her "kid" later and advise him of my thoughts on the using and abusing of his faithful old mother.) The woman seemed satisfied and shortly after went on her way.

Someone once said – I believe it was Washington Irving:

In bad repute, in the face of the world's condemnation, a mother's love lives on. She still hopes that her child will turn from evil ways and repent. She remembers his infant smiles and the joys of his childhood, the opening promise of his youth, and she cannot be brought to think of him as unworthy.

Well said! Sometimes even a hardened prison warden can learn a dramatic fact.

THE AMAZING MR. BECKSTEAD

I never saw a man who looked with such a wistful eye
Upon that little tent of blue that prisoners call the sky.
- Oscar Wilde

The title "the amazing Mr. Beckstead" was attached by *Denver Post* reporter John Snyder to a prisoner (Paul Beckstead) serving a life sentence in the prison. John and I were friends for many years, and he was one of the talented journalists of the 1950s and 1960s who died young. His hobby was writing crime stories for magazines such as *True Detective* and others of this type. John visited me often while I was Warden, and he interviewed many prisoners while constructing his stories. (The pseudonym he wrote under was "Luke Frost," and I suspect some of his narratives are still around.)

"John, how did you arrive at this title for Beckstead?" I asked him one day.

"Pat," he replied, "I've talked to Beckstead and studied his record for several years. He is some sort of a perverted genius. He plans crimes and escape plots with endless patience, down to every detail, and executes them by the book – to the dotting of the last 'i'. Some prisoners see themselves as escape artists, but he is the real thing. Don't let him out of sight."

Beckstead had been arrested at the Denver airport preparing to flee to Atlanta. He had left a rented car parked at the airport garage, and an airport security officer had called the police when he had detected a bad odor emanating from the trunk of the automobile. The police opened the trunk, found the dead and decaying body of an unknown man and apprehended Beckstead before the plane could depart. Subsequently, Beckstead was tried for murder in the first degree and sentenced to life in the Colorado State Penitentiary.*

My first meeting with Paul Beckstead was while I was the Warden at Buena Vista, the Colorado Men's Reformatory. Since the inmates there were mostly young men with no work experience, we transferred prisoners on trusty status from the penitentiary to do jobs requiring some skill. The Buena Vista facility had no hospital (only a three-bed infirmary), and a doctor came from nearby Salida three times a week and in emergencies. Tom Lee, a male nurse, supervised the infirmary, and he requested that a medical technician be recruited from the penitentiary to assist him.

I called Warden Harry Tinsley at the territorial prison, and told him of several jobs that we had open where we could use convicts. A medical technician was among these. "I've got a good medical tech, name of Beckstead," Tinsley said, "and he has asked to be considered."

Thus, I came to interview the "amazing Mr. Beckstead." He was a mature man of average build, good looking with hair graying at the temples and a very convincing speaker. In citing his qualifications, he was very reassuring as to his abilities. Harry Tinsley gave Beckstead a good endorsement, so I authorized his transfer.

Immediately, Beckstead became an important addition to the Buena Vista infirmary. Tom Lee was delighted with his services, and Dr. Smith began to depend on him helping with

---

* At the same time, police found another rented car with a dead man in the trunk, but the two deaths were never connected.

minor surgery and other important duties. I became involved in other aspects of reformatory administration and lost track of both Tom's and Mr. Beckstead's activities although I received good reports on our medical program. (If we humans could only be endowed with more foresight than hindsight!)

One day I was away from the institution and in Kremmling attending the funeral of State Trooper George Meyers, an old friend of mine, when Deputy Warden Douglas called and said, "Tom Lee and Beckstead left for Salida to buy some drugs and supplies and they have disappeared."

"Who authorized Beckstead outside?" I asked.

"You did," the deputy replied. "The Director of Institutions ordered us to buy generic drugs, and Beckstead is the only one in the infirmary that knows anything about them. So you told me to let him go to help Tom with the drug-buying program."

"Okay," I said. "I'll be back shortly, so keep checking on them." (Oh, hindsight! I could see Lee dead, crammed in the trunk of the car.)

Hurrying back to the institution, I drove on the routes that the two men should have taken and watched for signs of any accident that may have sent them over an embankment. There were none, as well as no leads of any kind to the men's whereabouts.

I talked with Tom's wife, who had no knowledge of the trip but did tell me that Tom trusted Beckstead. Still, I had visions of Tom dead in the trunk. He had been trained in hospitals, had no previous experience in a prison setting and had been employed at the reformatory only six months prior to this event. With the exception of calls to law enforcement officials, there seemed to be nothing we could do as we had no idea where to search for the missing men.

However, my Monday morning mail galvanized everyone into action. A letter postmarked Albuquerque contained, in substance, the following:

Warden:

Lee is handcuffed to a tree exactly 25 miles north of the city limits of Santa Fe. You better get to him fast as he will be in bad shape. I left him there Friday at noon. Sorry, but I couldn't do any more time.

Paul

The watermark on the stationery was that of a major airline. We had a lead!

I notified the F.B.I. and sped for Albuquerque. Raymond Rey, my administrative assistant, took a map and calculated twenty-five miles north of Santa Fe. When the two of us neared a "pullout" in the road, we were flagged down by a group of citizens from Tres Piedras, New Mexico, and they took us to a restaurant in Tres Piedras where Tom Lee was seated eating breakfast. I breathed easier as he appeared to be in good shape except for some scratches on his arms and legs.

Lee explained that during the trip to Salida, Beckstead had a sudden, drastic urge to relieve himself. Lee braked to a quick stop at a road pullout, and Beckstead scurried out of sight over an embankment. Shortly, he returned with an automatic pistol and handcuffs. He handcuffed Lee, took over the driving to New Mexico and, at a fairly isolated spot, handcuffed Lee to a tree about 300 yards off the road in dense timber. Beckstead told Lee that he would notify the warden in Colorado where to find him.

Lee spent the next two days trying to free himself from a twenty-foot tall tree about eight inches in diameter. Luckily, three New Mexico men stopped at the pullout to relieve themselves and heard Lee calling. The men cut down the tree to free Lee and took him to Tres Piedras.

Loading Lee into our car, we continued on to Albuquerque, located the airline office where the letter to me had been written and found the State car in an adjacent garage. Then

26

we reached a dead end. The "amazing Mr. Beckstead's" trail disappeared. If he had boarded a plane, this had been done under an assumed name.

Some two years later, the F.B.I. brought me a P38 automatic pistol* and told me that it was taken from Beckstead when he was arrested in a small Louisiana town as he exited a motel after a stickup. The agent said Beckstead had been convicted and sentenced to five years in the federal prison in Atlanta.

When Beckstead's federal sentence had been served, he was returned to Cañon City to continue his life sentence and was assigned to the prison library. By then I had left the reformatory and, as Warden at the prison, I conducted several interviews with Beckstead to see if he could fill in some of the "unknowns" of the Buena Vista escape. The talks were cordial but unproductive. Beckstead declined to discuss any of his past but did make the comment, "Warden, I suppose I'm here forever as far as you are concerned, with no job outside the walls."

"Yes," I replied. "Except for legal release, you will only leave these walls in a box."

Oh! How wrong my tough talk was! The "amazing Mr. Beckstead" wasn't done yet. He returned to his duty in the library, assumed a low profile and started a five-year, intricate plan to escape. The library had become a very important program in the prison, and Beckstead consulted independently with the State Librarian as to ordering books and then reported regularly to the Deputy and Associate Warden.

At the same time he was charming a homely little fifteen-year-old girl who was the sister of a fellow convict. She contended that she was nineteen, so none of the staff paid any

---

* I learned, after I made an internal investigation at the prison, that an officer of the institution had planted the gun and cuffs at the place where Tom and Beckstead had stopped on their way to Salida. The finding could never be proven, but the suspected officer was fired, with no appeal.

attention to what was happening. She wrote long letters to Beckstead, pledging her love and any help he might need to be released. (Apparently, the mail officers were asleep as they passed these letters without question.)

The timing of Beckstead's escape plan was nearing fruition. He approached the Deputy Warden to get permission to consult with the State Librarian. The deputy called me, and I ASSUMED that the consultation would be inside the prison, so I said, "Sure, no problem."

The following Monday, I was to meet for lunch in Denver with the Associate Warden. When I entered the restaurant, I thought I saw Beckstead heading for the restroom. Not believing my eyes, I turned around and the "amazing Mr. Beckstead" was gone!

It was later determined that Beckstead was picked up around the corner from the restaurant by his enamored girlfriend who was waiting at the exact time. He stayed with her for several days, dying his hair and trying to alter his appearance. Then, he abandoned her and contacted several "ex-con" friends to borrow money. Unfortunately, for him, a twenty dollar bill that he borrowed was bogus, and the police were looking for a car belonging to the forger. The "Amazing Mr. Beckstead" was going to the grocery store, armed and riding in the forger's car, when the police surrounded him. He had run out of escapes.

Apparently, Beckstead had to decide whether he would shoot it out with the officers or give himself up and be returned to prison to continue his interrupted life sentence. No one can know what thoughts were in his mind; however, he placed the gun barrel in his mouth and ended the story. (I was called to the morgue to identify him.)

Luke Frost (John Snyder) wrote one more story about the "Amazing Mr. Beckstead" and his demise for the pulp magazines. Frost ended his tale with this paragraph:

Mr. Beckstead spent most of his life pursuing liberty, escape from the control of others, and freedom, though he didn't want to be burdened with any obligations to retain them. His pursuit ended in a shady Denver side street with the barrel of a pistol in his mouth – He's now free.

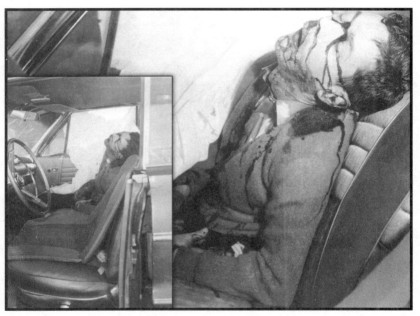

Photo of Beckstead sent to Warden Patterson by police.

Prison Boxing Team

*Boxing matches were held periodically on
the prison grounds. Matches were also
scheduled with boxers from outside the
institution, for example, Fort Carson.
Clifford Mattax was coach of the team
which had boxers in the featherweight,
middleweight, and heavyweight divisions.*

JOE SAM WALKER

When life is so burdensome;
death has become for man a sought-after refuge.
- Herodotus

In 1965, shortly after I came to the prison as Warden, a man came to my office and introduced himself as Jimmy McDonald, a private detective. He said he had been working for five years on the case of convicted murderer Joe Sam Walker (#25633). McDonald wanted to discuss the case with me and get permission to administer, or have administered, to Joe a series of lie detector and truth serum tests as part of an appeal he was perfecting to go back to the governor or the courts.

"I'll approve if that is the wish of Joe Sam," I said and had Joe brought to my office. At that time he was working in the large greenhouse inside the walls. Later, Joe was put in charge of the residential greenhouse outside the walls where I saw him and had occasion to talk with him on a regular basis.

I had known of Joe's case due to the extensive coverage of every phase of the crime and trial by *The Denver Post*.* The crime

---

* On November 11, 1998, in "This Day in History" in *The Denver Post* the case was again in the news: "The battered body of Theresa C. Foster, an 18 year old University of Colorado student was found 12 miles south of Boulder near Marshall." Then on the 23rd: "Information charging Joe Sam Walker, 31, Eldorado Springs metal worker, with murder in the slaying of Boulder coed Theresa Foster was lodged in the district court in Boulder."

was committed on November 9, 1948, on the farm property of a friend of my family, so it was of particular interest to me.

Joe agreed to take the tests, stating, "I've taken them before and nobody paid any attention, so I doubt if they will help. But Jimmy has worked on my case for many years, without any money, because he believes that I am innocent – and, Warden, I am!"

I sat in on one truth serum test and listened to the evidence that Detective McDonald had accumulated. Joe told his side of the story, and I became, with some reservations, convinced of his innocence as to the crime of murder. Detective McDonald was also a convincing asset underlining Joe's story. As best I can recall, his story went something like this:

I was living and working as a metal worker in Eldorado Springs. I lived with my wife and daughter in a spot off the highway in the canyon. On November 11, 1948, I drove into Boulder to pick up some cigarettes and some beer. I decided to stop and have a beer at a bar.

A young college girl carrying some books and school supplies sat down beside me, and we had a casual conversation. I continued to drink beer and talk. I don't recall if she had more than one beer. She finally asked me to drop her by her room in Boulder, and I agreed.

As we were leaving the bar, a big, blonde-headed boy came up to the car and engaged the girl in conversation. They seemed to know each other very well and were arguing. I was pretty drunk at that time, and they asked me to drive them to a place north of Boulder.

I agreed and they directed me to a place north of Boulder where we entered a farm gate and drove to a large isolated area with a turn-around and no exit. It was sort of a lovers' lane and known to the university kids. I got out of the car to relieve myself and walked to the front of the car – and that's all I remember until I woke up sometime later, bleeding from a severe head wound.

I got up and went to the car. There was no sign of the blonde man; the trunk of the car was open, and I saw the girl stuffed into the trunk – dead. I closed the trunk and decided that I would never escape this as I did not know the name of either person. I was still under the influence of the beer and with a bad wound on my head; so I decided to find a place to dispose of the body. I came to a bridge, stopped the car and pushed her body over the rail into the creek bed below. I then started to drive home, and I threw out the school books and papers by the roadside. I told the story to my wife, but she didn't believe me and threatened to go to the police. However, after thinking it over, she decided not to go that route after all.

The girl's body had been discovered the same day, November 11th. The following ten days were a circus as *The Denver Post* assigned a horde of reporters to cover the case, and each issue was covered with speculation about what had happened. Me and my car were connected to the girl's disappearance. I didn't dare to visit the doctor, and the wound on my head was infected. The reporters came to the house and then the police officers. I was arrested and jailed, and on November 23, 1948, I was charged with murder. The rest of the publicity was seemingly endless. When a lawyer was appointed and we appeared in court together, we were spat upon and threatened with lynching. Eventually I was convicted of second degree murder and given 80 years to life.

I continued to protest my innocence of this crime. I *did not* murder the girl, but the only person who took any interest in my case was Detective Jimmy. He said my wound occurred after being hit by a wrench – from behind!! He also located two old folks living down the road toward town from the murder site who said they saw a large man walking toward town at about that time of the evening, around the time of the murder. Nobody paid any attention to the old folks' story. Jimmy kept working but no results.

I believe that Detective McDonald's investigation caught the interest of a well-known attorney, Francis Salazar, and in 1965 he took Joe Sam's case back to the Boulder court. Salazar recounted the massive amount of pretrial publicity and other problems of the original trial, and in 1968 the court overturned the conviction and ordered Joe Sam's release. Joe Sam came into my office to tell me goodbye and he jokingly said, "Boss, I don't even get the twenty-five bucks you give to everyone turned out of here." I ordered clothing for him, and I gave him my personal check for twenty-five dollars.

Personally, I believe he was guilty of disposing of the body and covering up the circumstances, but I always had strong doubts that he committed murder.

After he was released, Joe Sam telephoned me once and indicated that he had a jewelry and watch repair job in Glenwood Springs. He was very depressed at that time and said:

> I sometimes wish I was back in the Pen. Everybody complimented me on my flowers and plants when I was working the greenhouse there (the penitentiary). Out here people complain all the time. If the repair is good, the price was too high. The boss knows my past and brings it up when someone complains. I'm beginning to think that freedom keeps requiring a lot of payback.

That's the last I heard from or about him until I received a call from Bill Gagnon of *The Pueblo Chieftain* informing me of Joe Sam's suicide in Waco, Texas.*

34

JOSHUA ARNOLD

There is a pleasure, sure, in being mad,
Which none but the madman knows.
                                        - Dryden

Joshua came to the prison on March 5, 1954, under a sentence of thirty to sixty years for the crime of aggravated robbery. From reports he appeared to have only a tenuous grasp on reality at that time and subsequently was transferred to the Colorado State Hospital at Pueblo and, after examination over a period of time, was found sane. Since he was an aggressive prisoner, he was again transferred to the prison for safekeeping. His mental condition, coupled with his aggressiveness, kept him in prison records regularly. Although he was always respectful when I talked with him, each day he would send scrawled notes, threatening me with dire consequences if I did not stop using radar to control his mind.

One morning the officer in charge of the mental unit advised me that Josh had asked for a typewriter in his cell. At first I said, "No." However, after a long discussion with the mental health authorities, I authorized his having the typewriter. Josh was delighted and immediately wrote me a series of letters complaining about my use of radar as a method of controlling his behavior. Again, he threatened reprisals if I did not cease the practice – forthwith. He did not confine his threats to me but also called on me to fire at least half of the prison officers for manning the "radar guns."

It seemed that Josh, adorned with black horn-rimmed glasses with no lenses, spent his entire daylight hours pounding on his machine. The barrage of mail was tolerated for it seemed to work as a cathartic and release for his physically aggressive temperament. Still, he took a paranoid view of the activities of all authorities in the prison, except for Lt. McDaniel who was in charge of the unit. Further, Josh threatened the officers in the towers who were "sending lightning bolts to harass him." He was, most of his waking hours, considered a classic case of what the mental experts called a paranoid schizophrenic.

On another morning, I was in my office reading the mail and I saw my usual letter from Josh. Thinking it was another threatening epistle spawned by his disordered mind, I laid it aside and did not read it until later in the afternoon. I finally read it – several times to be exact:

Warden Wayne K. Patterson
Wardens office
CSP

Deer* Warden:

I have just red in yesterdays paper that the Government agreeculture dept has set aside a million dollars for a study of the losses in the turkey industry. The story says that the hen turkeys do not set down when they lay thier eggs and the industry is losing millions of dollars because the eggs are broken from the drop. The eggs drop ten inches without any cushion of nesting material and 75% are broken. I have a

---

* This letter is reproduced with all of Joshua's spelling errors intact.

solution to the problem and I would appreciate it if you would forward my solution to the proper authorities and claim the million dollars for me. My solution is this: Build the floors in the turkey houses ten inches closer to the hen turkeys ass!!

Sincerely

Joshua A.

Now, readers. You be the judge. Was Joshua as crazy as I thought and as the doctors had reported??

Warden Patterson
with Actor John Forsythe

Forsythe was in Cañon City during the filming of the movie
In Cold Blood. *Based on the book of the same title by*
author Truman Capote, the prison scenes were filmed at
Territorial. Although the murders took place in Kansas,
and the perpetrators were sentenced in that state,
the Kansas prison system would not permit filming
in their institution.

"THE FIXER"

Justice, though moving at a tardy pace,
has seldom failed to overtake the wicked in their flight.
- Horace

The "fixer" arrived at the prison in the mid 1960s, after being convicted of procuring an abortion. Procuring appeared to be one of his "fixing" specialties. The reputation that came with him was that he could *"fix anything in his home county of Pueblo, Colorado for his friends – for a fee."*

Interestingly, the doctor who was convicted of performing the abortion for "the fixer" and his client arrived at the prison at the same time as he did. The doctor, who was in the final stages of cancer, was brought in on a stretcher, and I was called to the Intake Unit to review his condition. After speaking with the terminally ill man and the prison doctor, I arranged for the prisoner to be transferred to the State Hospital, where he died a few days later.

Since I was in the Intake Unit to check on the dying doctor, I decided I'd take a look at "the fixer." I had already had letters from friends of his in Pueblo attesting to his help in fixing everything from traffic tickets to alleged manslaughter. "The fixer" was a short, heavyset man with a perpetual, ingratiating grin on his face. He immediately "name dropped" a few of my friends in Pueblo County, intimating that they were close friends of his. He assured me that he would be no problem during his three-year sentence.

"The fixer's" record indicated that he was a fringe operator with some Mafia connections in his home county and showed several arrests, mostly for illegal gambling. He boasted that he knew all of the law enforcement officers, judges and other political people in the state. This was to let me know that (for free or a negotiable fee) he could fix anything for his friends or if someone was referred by a friend. I saw "the fixer" only a couple of times during the next year, usually when one of his *friends* sought special permission to visit him.

Nearly a year after "the fixer" was admitted, the prison doctor came to my office to report that "the fixer" had cancer of the throat and needed an immediate surgical procedure that the prison was unable to provide. I was also informed that the surgery could be performed at the University of Colorado hospital in Denver at a cost of twelve to fifteen hundred dollars. After a series of conferences with no viable alternatives, I agreed to the procedure. Two weeks later, "the fixer" was back at the prison with no ability to speak and a huge bandage around his throat. When the prisoner became ambulatory, I had him assigned to the prison garden where he could have an easy job feeding the chickens and gathering eggs while he recovered fully from the surgery. I thought I could go back to my business of running the prison minus any interruptions concerning "the fixer," but it was not to be.

My morning mail brought a three-page letter, containing many medical terms, from a Dr. Black at the university hospital. It described the surgery on "the fixer" and indicated that very shortly he would need another resection of the other side of his neck. Further, it indicated that his illness had invaded his lymph glands and was considered terminal. Since he was serving a three-year term, it appeared that the prison was faced with several expensive surgeries and, shortly, the death of "the fixer."

40

I called "the fixer" into my office and gave him the bad news. "Warden," he said, speaking in a barely audible, hoarse whisper, "I already knew that I was a goner, and I appreciate all you've done."

The next week I received a large amount of mail from "the fixer's" friends and relatives. All of the letters followed the same theme: We will look after him in his last days, and we have the funds to pay for any additional surgeries.

I got out Dr. Black's report and reread it. Obviously, it would be somewhat inhumane to allow a man to die in prison when he was serving a short term and had completed all of it except for one year. In addition, he apparently had money of his own, his family had resources to support him during his final days, and, lastly, his crime was of a nonviolent nature.

Still, keeping in mind that "the fixer" was a con man of long standing, I carefully reviewed all of the records and conducted a long interview with him to assure myself of the finality of his illness and to sympathize a bit as he faced a short, dark future. Also, I received more letters and telephone calls begging me to help him get released in order for him to die in the free world, among his friends and relatives. It was all very touching.

With humane thoughts in mind, I dictated a letter to Governor John Love, citing the entire facts – terminal illness, enthusiasm of friends and relatives, their financial ability to pay for needed medical attention and, finally, the savings to the State of Colorado taxpayers if his family assumed these future costs. I asked that his sentence be commuted to "time served" to allow his immediate release. Governor Love, a very thoughtful and humane man, responded by immediately commuting the sentence, and "the fixer" was released to spend his last days a free man. However, this was not the last of "the fixer"; there would be an epilogue to the story, which nearly caused me to have a bad case of ulcers!

41

Some two years later I was sorting through a large stack of mail when my secretary, Marie Goertz, came in to say, "A Mr. Fixer is waiting to see you."

"Send him in," I replied, puzzled by her announcement. To my surprise, who walked in but "the fixer."

He looked hale and hearty and my immediate reaction was, "You old bastard! You were supposed to die two years ago! You've double-crossed Governor Love and me by failing to die on schedule."

"The fixer" laughed and said, "Well, Warden, the Lord saved me, and I have been blessed by a full recovery." When I inquired as to his reason for needing to see me, he said, "I wanted to thank both you and the Governor for being so kind and thoughtful in my behalf."

I thought this comment was a little late in coming (over two years), so I asked what else had brought him to the prison.

"Warden, I need to see a prisoner by the name of Joe Smith," he began. "Joe was sent here by the judge to do a sentence of thirteen to fourteen years for transportation of marijuana. The judge says that if he could get some additional information, he would like to reduce his sentence; the judge asked me to talk to Smith and secure this information."

I began to smell a fix. "The fixer" was at it again. "Why would the judge ask *you*, of all people, to act in his behalf?"

"It's because I know Joe and was a witness at his trial," explained "the fixer," with an earnest expression on his face.

Finally, I agreed to allow "the fixer" to see Joe Smith, but I cataloged in my mind that *something smelled*. A few days later I received a call from an agent with the Colorado Bureau of Investigation (CBI) who made an appointment to talk with me the following day. The agent went immediately to the point. The Bureau was investigating the possible "shakedown" of one of the prisoners by the name of Joe Smith. This was being done by a judge with "the fixer" as the go-between. My hunch had been correct, and I advised the agent of the previous contact with prisoner Joe Smith by "the fixer."

The scenario as envisioned by the CBI agent was that the judge had given Smith a long sentence of thirteen to fourteen years with the idea that if Joe could come up with $5,000, the sentence would be cancelled and Smith would be given probation. The go-between was "the fixer." The plan was that I would alert the CBI if the amended sentence came through, and the Bureau would have Joe Smith carry out the payoff. Then the CBI would "net" both the judge and "the fixer."

A week later an amended mittimus arrived, cancelling Smith's previous long sentence and granting him probation. I called the CBI agent, and he picked up Joe and transported him away from the prison. Apparently the plan didn't work out in its entirety. The judge escaped the net because the law couldn't recover the money from the payoff, but "the fixer" was convicted of conspiracy to commit a felony. A grand jury sitting in Pueblo made inquiry into the case and indicted "the fixer," who was tried in Colorado Springs. I was summoned to testify in the case, and "the fixer" greeted me in front of the crowd as if I were a long lost brother. (He wasn't so enthusiastic after I testified.) The facts of the trial indicated that Joe Smith had been "wired" when he met "the fixer" at the Colorado Springs airport. Joe handed over $2,000 in cash of the intended $5,000 and promised more later. Since the lawmen were unable to follow the money, the case ended with "the fixer." The judge was never identified, and "the fixer" went back to the penitentiary for two more years.

With all the attendant publicity, the politicians and later a grand jury began to question how "the fixer" had gotten out of prison on the previous sentence before it was completely served. The press thought this was a good question and began to look to the governor; he, in turn, looked to the warden for the answer. I called on the files for Dr. Black's letter of the surgeries and the *terminal* cancer. BUT no letter could be found! It had mysteriously disappeared from the prison files.

I posted a letter to the CU Hospital requesting a copy of the letter written three years earlier by a Dr. Black. To my great relief, a copy of the letter from Dr. Black to me was produced and made public, with favorable results. Governor Love's and my humane concerns in "the fixer's" case were vindicated. However, being a warden can sometimes contribute to severe indigestion – if not ULCERS!

PRESIDENT AND CEO
OF THE "FAST BUCK"
Henri P. Karr

He could not discern the legal line between
sharp business and confidence game.
-WKP

My first encounter with Henri Karr occurred in the spring of 1953 when I interviewed him regarding his parole. I read with much interest the story of the crime for which he was convicted and was given a two to three-year term.

During a bad cold spell in 1951, Henri and his wife arrived in Greeley, Colorado. He stopped at a filling station to service his car – a custom-made Cadillac with his name on the dashboard. Henri was an imposing looking man in his early fifties, wearing a shiny, silk-looking dark suit. He was about five feet nine inches tall, of ordinary build with salt and pepper hair that extended over his collar in a sweeping mane.* His wife, a "classy-looking" woman, complimented his appearance.

---

* The reason I go to such lengths to describe Henri is that his victims could only describe him in general terms and had trouble identifying him in later lineups. Some said he looked like a very, very successful business man; some thought he was some movie actor; some said oil man. When questioned, they could not say which actor he resembled. Some said he smoked large cigars and sported several rings which appeared very expensive.

In casual conversation with the station owner, Karr learned that there was a severe shortage of anti-freeze. The owner explained that the shortage was state wide and that wholesalers could not promise any relief in the foreseeable future. "I'm being besieged by regular customers needing anti-freeze for the winter," the station owner complained, "and I simply can't get any."

That evening in his motel room, Henri P. Karr organized a company – The Frost Proof Chemical Company. Early the next morning he arrived at a local print shop and ordered a pad of order sheets with the Frost Proof name next to the logo of a barrel of antifreeze and a Chicago address and phone number. He told the printer that he was in a hurry and needed a twenty-page proof pad by noon. Picking up the proof pad, he told the printer that he would be back later in the afternoon to confirm a large print order.

Pad in hand, Henri canvassed the town writing up orders for antifreeze by the barrel, with a two-week delivery time. The product was cheap – $110 for a 55-gallon drum. By that evening he had sold a carload of antifreeze, giving every customer a receipt for their money. The stations and dealers were delighted when two weeks later barrels of beautiful blue antifreeze began to arrive. They sold out immediately. However, when they tried to call the Chicago phone number to reorder, they found the phone had been disconnected. They tried to locate Henri to place further orders but realized they didn't know his name, and he could not be found in town.

The dealers again resigned themselves to the fact that antifreeze would be in short supply for the rest of the winter. Then trouble started! A farmer who used the antifreeze called a service station stating that his pickup had "froze up" and cracked and had ruined the radiator. Another said his tractor froze; still another indicated he was contemplating a lawsuit as his personal car had been ruined. Complaints ballooned, and a group of victims threatened to sue the corporation who had manufactured the faulty product. In anticipation of the lawsuit, the antifreeze was tested. It turned out to be a *weak solution of salt water and blue food coloring*!

The District Attorney began a search for the perpetrators, but there was no such corporation as Frost Proof Chemical Company in Chicago. The only clue was the receipts that Karr had issued, but the printer could not describe Henri who had not returned after getting the original proof pads. Fortunately, the first service station operator remembered that the Cadillac had a plaque on the dashboard that stated, "This car was custom built for Henri P. Karr."

An arrest warrant was issued for Henri which gave only a confusing description of the man but a good description of his car. Shortly thereafter, he was arrested in Denver and returned to Greeley for trial. His defense – that he sold the antifreeze in good faith, but the shipper in Chicago was responsible for the bad product. Victims packed the courtroom and suggested hanging would be too good for Henri, but since he had no previous criminal record, the judge gave him a three-to-five-year sentence in the penitentiary.

His wife, a very refined and loyal lady, visited him regularly. Henri proved to be a very affable, cooperative prisoner and was released on parole after his first appearance before the Parole Board. His first job on parole was promoting the "Little Britches" Rodeo in Arapahoe County. However, the appointment was terminated by the director of the rodeo when they became dissatisfied with the amount and usage of funds paid by advertisers. (It seemed the funds were equally divided – one half to the rodeo and one half to Henri P. Karr.) He then obtained a job as a traveling salesman for a very reputable firm in Denver.

The reader must realize that to his parole agent, Karr was considered a minimum risk. He faithfully reported to the agent monthly, giving an account of his activities. As he had a job which required him to travel, he was issued a travel permit with instructions as to reporting in other states. At that time the Parole

Department was supervising about 2,100 parolees with ten agents, and Henri was lost in the paper work. I was the Executive Director of parole at that time, and I had a long talk with Henri before his release. Other than that I *assumed* that he was on the straight path to good citizenship. My *assumption* turned bad and adversely affected several dozen businesses in several states.

Some months after his parole, I received a call from an Assistant District Attorney in Oklahoma City. In only a few words, he explained the problem.

A parolee named Karr has checked in with the Oklahoma parole office, as required by the interstate compact. He said he was President of The Plantan Peanut Company with offices in Oklahoma City, Tulsa and Fort Smith, Arkansas. Trouble is Planters Peanut Company has made inquiries with the Better Business Bureau indicating that someone was selling an inferior product and using a logo that duplicated theirs. They want to pursue a lawsuit if the man can be found.

I asked the Assistant D.A. to send me copies of the sales slips, business cards, address and phone numbers and we would investigate. Calling the first phone number given me by the D.A., I found the address was Suite 220 at the Muelbach Hotel in Kansas City. The secretary who answered the phone said that she knew very little about Henri.

"He is a very imposing-looking man," she ventured. "I'm paid ten dollars a week to forward his mail to his current address."

She further offered that his address "changed terribly often" and told me that she thought his current address was in Sayre, Oklahoma. When I asked her why she thought Henri needed a "drop," she said she thought he wanted to "sound big and impressive with her address" which was a large law firm occupying one half of the entire floor in the hotel. (We also found that Henri had several other mail drops at prestigious-sounding addresses.)

Continuing with our investigation, we learned that for the "Plantan peanut operation," Henri bought peanuts in bulk in Sayre, had small bags printed with the Planter's logo,* stapled the bags to a counter display and sold these to every store, restaurant, service station and rest stop in about five surrounding states. From the testimony of buyers, it appeared to be 150% profit for Henri, who would sell you a two-ounce bag or a truck load – if the price was right! A phone call to his Denver employer revealed that Henri had been dismissed several weeks earlier, but no reason was given. As we dug deeper, we discovered that Henri had several other "con games" going.

Finally, he was arrested, and I suspended his parole and returned him to the prison for a Parole Board hearing. However, there were so many shady areas in the investigation of the "con games" that the Board gave him the benefit of the doubt and reinstated his parole. The Board did specify that he remain in Colorado, report every week and establish a permanent residence. He did as the Board specified, finally completed his sentence and was discharged.

For months after his release, those of us in the parole office were kept busy answering inquiries from sheriffs, D.A.s and Better Business Bureaus about Henri. Letters kept coming indicating that he was up to more mischief – but he still had *only one entry on his criminal record.* Eventually we were able to identify the following "organizations" which Henri had set up:

No Freeze, Inc.
123 N. Howard St.
Chicago, Illinois
Henri P. Karr, Pres. and CEO
(No such place – sold antifreeze by the case)

---

* The logo on Henri's Plantan Peanut Company was nearly identical to the Planter's Company logo – same colors with Mr. Peanut and his cane. The only difference was the spelling.

Frost Proof Chemical Co.
14560 Outer Drive
Chicago, Illinois
(Dealt in bogus antifreeze by the barrel. Showed
no corporate names on this one.)

Plantan Peanut Co.
Henri P. Karr, Pres. and CEO
Sayre, Oklahoma
(Dealt in second-grade peanuts.)

Globe Lighting Co.
Henri P. Karr, CEO
Suite 418 Cosmopolitan Hotel
Denver, Colorado
(Don't know what was being sold here.)

Gloves Unlimited
Henri P. Karr, Prop.
Suite 220 Muelbach Hotel
Kansas City, Missouri
(Nothing on what happened here.)

The Bug Medicine Man
Henri P. Karr, Prop.
Suite 220 Muelbach Hotel
Kansas City, Missouri
(Stapled a felt cloth about six inches by six inches
to a display card with logo of bug man wiping a
streak across a windshield loaded with mashed
bugs. Cost was a dollar because of the chemical in
the cloth.)

Hand Opener, Inc.

"Easy Grasp Co." (On the letterhead)
Henri P. Kane, Pres. and CEO
Henry Marten, Vice Pres.
1460 State Street
Oklahoma City, Oklahoma
(Had an invention of a handle that would open a beer can and then serve as a handle to allow drinking from the can. The logo looked like a Coors beer can, but it was called "Cool Beer". This was before "fliptop" cans. I surmise that he sucked another person into this, for the financing.)

Blue Ice Cream Co.

Wabash and First Street
Chicago, Illinois
Happy Kane, CEO
(Don't know what was sold here but no such business at the address listed.)

Henri P. Karr was an amazing "con man." He could organize a corporation in ten minutes and have it in full operation in one hour. He always needed to have his name on all organizational papers, and if he is still alive, he will be thinking in terms of the suckers out there – sheep waiting to be shorn – while none seem to remember his name or even what he looked like.

Captured!

Associate Warden Carl Douglas (in plaid shirt)
directed the capture of inmates Dolan and York
at Castle Rock Ranch. They were on the run for
two or three days after crashing a truck
through the east gate fence. Both men were
originally sentences for stick-ups and burglary.

THE MAN WITH THE "BALL-BEARING" EYES

John Roger Knight

He who comes from the kitchen, smells of smoke.
                                              -Lavitor

John Roger was afflicted with some type of physical problems that caused his bulging eyes to rotate in opposite directions. He had adjusted to this problem by loving life and being full of self-deprecating jokes and stories. A short, stout black man about thirty years old, he was a petty type of offender and had traveled all over the country, living in religious missions and in downtown "flop houses" – anywhere there was food and a cot for sleeping. Always on the move, if he found night coming and he was in a farming community, he charmed any watch dogs and slept in the hay loft. If luck held, he'd steal a few eggs and leave before dawn.

If John got caught, he would usually charm the farmer and have the man laughing and feeding him at the back door before sending him on his way. Unfortunately, at one place John carried away a ham from the farmer's smokehouse. Apparently the farmer had no sense of humor (and maybe a penchant for white sheets with eye holes cut in the headpiece), and he called the authorities. John Roger got a five-to-ten-year sentence in Cañon City. While he was confined, John ended up with two nicknames – "the man with the ball bearing eyes" and "Stereo." Penitentiary officers called him by number, some convicts called him "Stereo" but no one seemed to know his real name. Still, everyone knew of his fun and jokes.

Eventually, I interviewed John Roger for parole, as I was Executive Director of Parole at that time. He had an aunt in California who volunteered to house him, *if he worked*. He was paroled and took his fun and laughs with him, leaving a vacuum within the old gray walls. He secured a job near his aunt in northern California and was to be supervised by agents of the California Parole Department. But John Roger couldn't hold a job and reverted to his old method of living. We (the Colorado Parole Department) were notified that John had absconded, and California officials asked that we issue a warrant and return him to Colorado, if he were arrested.

Shortly, we heard that John was being held in the county jail in Fresno, California. He had waived extradition, so we sent two agents to return him to Colorado. At that time I was attending a meeting in Sacramento and told the two agents that I would fly into Fresno, meet them and ride home with them. (I was trying to conserve state money, but *that was a serious mistake* as the next few days demonstrated.)

Upon arriving at the Fresno airport, I found the agents waiting with John in the backseat of their auto. On his left leg, from his toes to his hip, was a filthy cast inscribed with the names of all of the prisoners in the Fresno jail. His toes, sticking out of the case were also filthy and smelled as if the cast were occupied by a family skunks. John was delighted to see me and to be free of the jail.

"Boy-o-boy, Mr. Patterson, am I glad to see you," he shouted, and the eyes rolled up.

"I'm sorry, John, but I can't say the same about you," I said, attempting to move back from the odor emanating from his leg.

I began to visualize riding 1,000 miles or more with John's leg cast in someone's lap – possibly mine! Finally, I decided that drastic measures were necessary, and we went to the local police headquarters where I explained our plight. A couple of officers took us to the car wash in the alley, and the two agents took turns hosing John. By the time they were finished, it was night and we all went to a motel. Now the big question! Who has to sleep in the same room with John? I felt sorry for the agents who had been with him long before I arrived, so we drew straws, with John Roger holding the straws. *I lost!*

I had purchased a powerful air freshener and sprayed both John and the room and opened the windows, but it was still a struggle to breathe. As we settled in for the night, he explained to me what had happened on his parole, his eyes rolling all through the story.

John had been fired from his job in northern California and headed south, staying in flop houses and "hobo jungles" until the welfare people assigned him to a work camp located on top of an old dump full of used tires and rusted car parts. He and other men lived in tents of twelve persons each and were assigned to pick cotton.

You was assigned the inside of two rows, and you was supposed to clean the inside of both rows, dragging a huge sack behind you. I was slow doing this, and the other two pickers on each side reached through the leaves and picked my side. When we got to the end of the row, they had their sacks half full, and I had almost nothin'.

That was okay with me until the boss man said, "You with the big eyeballs better pick more or you go back to the jail." That really scared me so I challenged the other two pickers to leave my cotton for me or they were in for a fight.

However, the two pickers continued to grab the cotton from the rows assigned to John, so the next day he decided to fight the pair. At first he was holding his own until he caught his foot in an old car wheel and broke his leg. The result was that John was arrested and told the police that he was a parole violator from Colorado. But he got his leg fixed, and I couldn't help laughing as he finished telling the story.

The four of us rode back to Colorado, taking turns riding in the backseat with John Roger's leg cast across our laps. Whenever possible, we held him overnight in jails across the country and got the sheriffs to periodically get him bathed. John entertained us and kept us laughing at his stories of the seamy side of life. When we checked him in at the prison, "the man with the ball bearing eyes" was thoroughly at home. The old time prisoners were glad to see him back as he brought some light and laughter into a place which held little hope.

I was very fond of John Roger Knight and took time to talk and laugh with him on my trips to the prison, although he was no longer eligible for a second parole.

JOHN SMALLEY

He does not die a death of shame
On a day of dark disgrace,
Nor have a noose about his neck
Nor a cloth upon his face
Nor drop feet foremost through the floor
Into an empty space.

Oscar Wilde

John Smalley came to the penitentiary on March 27, 1929, and by his own words had only fifty-nine days of freedom from March 9, 1929, through 1964. He served three sentences and he grinned when he said in 1964, "A few of those fifty-seven days of freedom were gained in a slightly illegal manner." Then, he went on to explain:

I have served on my present sentence twenty-four years and six months. More than ten years of this twenty-four was spent in solitary confinement. Not a straight ten years – I served twenty-nine months and ten days, thirty-three months and fourteen days and five years, four months and eight days for a total of 127 months and one day. This totals up to ten years, seven months and one day.

I might add that the first ordeal of twenty-nine months was under the most trying conditions. Among a multitude of other minor cruelties, for the first twenty-four months of that twenty-nine, I did not have a bath, and it was sometimes as long as six months between changes of clothing.

In his early days as a criminal actor, John was an enigma. A short, stocky man, he had a thoroughly disarming grin and an agreeable, outgoing personality. Behind the grin, however, was a very dangerous man during his middle years. As can be seen from his own comments above, John was in constant trouble during his long period in prison. He escaped once and continually attempted other escapes. John told me that Captain Chet Yeo checked *every* day for a year to be certain he was in his cell. Captain Yeo said that John was a grasshopper, jumping always in the same direction – out the gate!

In addition to the attempted escapes, John smuggled marijuana into the institution and smoked it.* He was a master metal worker, adept at making knives – not just penitentiary "shanks" but jackknives with multiple blades that opened and closed. He was often on report and confined to solitary for various things he did or was suspected of doing. He accepted his punishment with good humor and a grin, even if he thought it was wrong. And he *was* punished! He was spanked many times on the "Old Gray Mare" and was a regular occupant of the "hole" and solitary confinement.

I first met up with John in 1942 while I was a State patrolman assigned as driver for Governor Ralph Carr, and we detoured from Salida to the prison after a report of a bombing. While the governor was talking to Warden Roy Best, I was taken to the prison morgue by Captain Bill Kinney and shown the body of a convict who had been blown in two by the bomb explosion. Captain Kinney showed me a duplicate bomb (unexploded) that had been found in the rain trough over the metal shop. Then we

---

* In one instance, the marijuana was smuggled into the prison by his sister as canned salmon. An informer caused the officers to find the contraband before it got to John.

Bomb That Killed Two Prisoners

The trigger mechanism was made by intricate steelwork. and John Smalley was a master at small steelwork, knives, etc. He was suspected of having designed and built this bomb, but he always denied it and grinned.

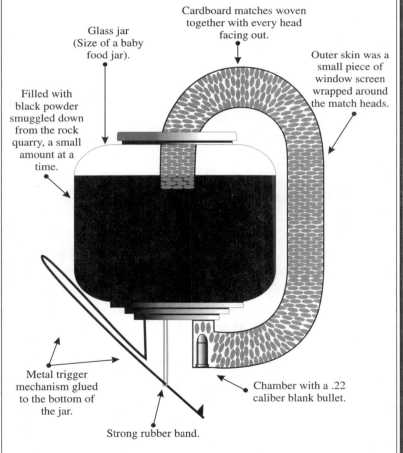

Cardboard matches woven together with every head facing out.

Glass jar (Size of a baby food jar).

Outer skin was a small piece of window screen wrapped around the match heads.

Filled with black powder smuggled down from the rock quarry, a small amount at a time.

Metal trigger mechanism glued to the bottom of the jar.

Chamber with a .22 caliber blank bullet.

Strong rubber band.

The bomber walked up to the victim, handed him the bomb, tripped the trigger and ran. The victim did not react to the gift until it was too late. The trigger fired the blank .22 and ignited the match heads, detonating the black powder.

went to the segregation unit where a grinning John Smalley was being held as a suspect in both making the bomb and doing the bombing. For years afterward, John always denied the charge – usually with a good-natured grin.

John's last big escapade was the 1947 escape* from Cell House #6, known as "Little Siberia." John didn't get far as he was caught in the Garden Park area of Cañon City after he was shot by pursuing officers. The bullet entered his lower back and exited through his gonads. He was hauled in misery into the prison in the back of a small jeep – but grinning. According to John, Warden Roy Best met him at the gate and when told of the prisoner's injury said, "You've never needed them, John, and you won't need them from now on."

After recovering from his wounds, John spent the next five years in solitary confinement, and the reader needs to have a description of this particular unit. Located on the north wall, the building was of stone construction with a gravel and dirt floor and was connected to other shops also located along the north wall. Ten small cells were built back-to-back in the center of the structure with an eight-foot walkway around the cell fronts. There was one lamp hanging over the center of the room with approximately a 100-watt bulb. There were no windows or outside light, and the cell fronts (red brick masonry up to about three feet with bars to the height of about seven feet and topped by six inches of concrete) all faced rock walls. Circulation of air in the building from a ceiling fan was minimal. The entry, locked from the outside, was a solid door with a small, barred view panel. Inside the entry and to the immediate right was a dilapidated old overstuffed chair for the on-duty officer. The "silent system" was enforced by threat of the "Old Gray Mare." There was no reading material, of course, as there was no light by which to read. Once

---

* This mass escape through the north gate in a severe snow storm was the true story line for the movie "Cañon City." See story, "Last Days of a Troubled Life."

a week prisoners were taken individually outside for a shower and clothing change.

In 1951, I had occasion to visit the solitary unit with Roy Best. When we entered the building, I noticed a slight tapping sound and asked George Winters, the Duty Officer accompanying us what it was.

"They are talking to each other," he explained. "They talk about six hours every day."

Later on John told me that the prisoners had developed their own code and communicated in solitary by tapping on the plumbing. With the aid of the code, they were aware that the Warden and I were the people in the unit right after we passed the first cell.

As we passed one cell, a convict named Hielman fell to his knees and with hands on the bars pleaded with Best. "Please, please let me out of here. *I can't do any more of this time!*"

"Well, Richard, you will just have to do what you can of it," Best replied, and we passed on to the next cell.

One cell on the west side was empty because the prisoner (Swartzmiller) had spent several months removing the mortar from the bricks in the front of his cell and replacing it with a combination of toilet paper and soap. By the time this clever ruse was discovered, the entire front was ready to be kicked out. One could look straight at the false front Swartzmiller had constructed and never believe that it wasn't really brick and mortar.

John just grinned when we passed his cell. "No parole, Mr. P.?" he asked.

Smalley finally completed his five-year solitary sentence, and by that time Warden Best was gone and Harry Tinsley had become Warden. The Old Gray Mare had been consigned to history.[*] Although John continued to be locked up, he was allowed to read books and converse with other prisoners. He began to read everything he could find – books on crime, history,

Greek mythology and psychology. Then Warden Tinsley appointed a "paid" school teacher to start voluntary classes for inmates to obtain a high school diploma through the GED (General Education Development) program. John joined up, completed that course and spent the next three years studying college courses as professors from various colleges and universities came to the prison to conduct classes. John became extremely well educated and made some friends among the university faculty, who took an interest in his background and history.

In the late 1950s, Warden Tinsley decided to start John on a "decompression cycle," a term applied to the process of preparing inmates who had done long terms for eventual parole. Tinsley asked me to transfer him to the Buena Vista reformatory where I had become Warden in the spring of 1958. At first I viewed the transfer of John as a calculated gamble, but since I had known him in the past, I decided to take the risk. John was delighted and very grateful.

Tyler Wright, a retired officer who maintained strong ties with the reformatory, took a special interest in John. Mr. Wright came to me one day and said, since he was both a source and had an active interest in the reformatory's history, that he would like to go through old records and put together a history of the institution. I agreed and he asked if he could use John in this endeavor. Together they researched and organized a pretty accurate reformatory history. (Later, Mr. Wright was appointed to the State Parole Board but was killed in an auto accident before he could serve.)

John was allowed to appear before the Parole Board and was paroled in the early 1960s. During his time in the prison, he

---

* During the Denver trial of Roy Best and seven staff officers for depriving prisoners of their civil rights by spanking them, a subpoena had been issued for the "Old Gray Mare." However, it had been dismantled and burned in the prison furnace.

had established some relationships with professors at Adams State College, Pueblo Junior College and Western State College and secured a position lecturing on criminality at Adams State. He was returned to the prison once for smoking "pot" with the college kids, but was re-released and was given a position at the University of Utah in a position similar to the one at Adams State.

That was the last I ever heard of John Smalley, except through some common sources. When I remember him, I never cease to wonder how this man was able to keep a remnant of sanity during his long, long prison life. John was a textbook case in his search for freedom. He lived through several violent prison uprisings, several escape attempts and spent an incredible time in harsh solitary confinement. However, when he finally attained freedom, his later life, apparently, was productive. (Colorado State Representative Jenkins told me that John was last heard of in San Diego in 1985, writing a book.)

Captain Chet Yeo (middle) watching the movie "Cañon City" with inmate John Smalley (left) and another inmate.

*Warden Patterson on Redbird
surveying the prison farm and ranch.*

*The prison farm (by the Abbey) consisted of 160
acres. The Castle Rock Ranch covered 5,000
acres and at any given time there were one
hundred to one hundred twenty-five cattle
grazing on the ranch. Aproximately one hundred
"trusty" inmates lived in the ranch bunkhouse,
overseeing the heard or working the dairy that
was located on the ranch.*

THE SAGA OF ROY AND JIMMY

There seemed to be a demand in those days for men
who could make wrong appear right.
-paraphrase of Terence, Pharmio

On December 15, 1947, an eleven-year-old boy named James Melton, Jr. took aim with a .22 rifle and fired five bullets into the back and head of his fifteen-year-old sister. The murder took place in the small southeastern Colorado town of Las Animas and made headlines all over the country. Records indicate that James Melton died in the Los Angeles area at age fifty. This time there were no headlines. Between these two records lies a strange story that I played a role in – first as an observer and then as an active participant in a prison experiment authored by a crusty, hardened prison warden with a caring, humane nature. Unfortunately, the experiment was a failure.

On December 16, 1947, James Melton, Jr. was questioned. He told police that two masked men had beaten him and kidnaped his sister, Phyllis. Later on, he confessed to the murder of Phyllis and was quoted as saying that "I never liked her." He was arrested and charged with murder the next day.

After a series of sanity tests, "Jimmy" pleaded guilty to second degree murder and was sentenced by Judge Herschel Horn to twelve years to life. He was taken to the prison February 25, 1948, fingerprinted, mugged, assigned number 24939 and then taken to Warden Roy Best's home outside the prison walls.

Later Roy told me, "Pat, I just couldn't put that boy inside the walls. I'm going to see if we can't let him serve his sentence with Mabel* and me in our home."

Roy Best was a real paradox as he was perceived by the public, the prisoners, his friends and his enemies. His friends saw him as a rough, fun-loving, thoughtful and caring man who controlled a den of animals. They and the public knew he would be on hand to defend the citizenry when the siren began to wail and the floodlights came alive.

His enemies saw him as an arrogant, corrupt man – a powerful political person with governors and legislators "in his hip pocket." They felt he was the warden who controlled his prisoners by flogging and brutality, a practice that had been abandoned for many years by every other prison administrator in the United States.

The prisoners seemed to be equally divided; some viewed him as sadistic and brutal, and personally did most of the flogging.** Other prisoners were very loyal and supportive of his operation of the prison.

Regardless of how Best was viewed by the world, his attempts to rescue Jimmy Melton from the dangerous and deleterious effects of life in prison were the best example of Roy's "other side." He took the boy into his home and treated him like a son. Roy had Jimmy enrolled in the Cañon City public schools but met such resistance from the community that he hired a private tutor, a Mrs. Heath, to assist Mabel in schooling the young man. Sadly, Mabel became ill and died, which broke a strong tie for Jimmy as she had become a mother figure for him. (Jimmy's real mother had divorced his father and was living in California at

_____

* Roy Best's first wife.

** Once when Best returned to his office after a session of spanking on "the old gray mare," he told me, "Every once in a while I have to take this prison back from the convicts." (See my additional comments at the end of this tale.)

the time of the murder.) Mabel's death seemed to destroy the family relationship that had been a part of the Best household.

As things in the home began to deteriorate, Roy Best appealed to Father Flannigan's Boys' Town in Omaha, Nebraska, to take Jimmy into their program. In a letter of support to Boys' Town, Best wrote, "He's been like a son to me and has done nothing to shake our faith in him during the six months he has lived with us."

Colorado Governor Lee Knous conditionally commuted Jimmy's sentence, and Jimmy became a resident of Boys' Town on March 26, 1949. The governor's commutation of sentence required that Jimmy remain in Boys' Town or the commutation would be withdrawn. Then, on September 23, 1949, Jimmy was returned to the prison in Cañon City after being captured in Council Bluffs, Iowa. He had hidden in the back of a visitor's car at Boys' Town, hit the driver over head with a lead pipe and stolen the man's auto. This time Jimmy was placed *behind* the walls and his commutation revoked.

Although I had visited with Jimmy before, I interviewed him when he became eligible for parole in 1953.* He was eighteen at that time, a small, thin man with thick glasses and a blank look on his face which gave the impression that he was not interested in anything I might have to say to him. His responses to my questions was, "Yes," "No" or "I don't know."

Jimmy was paroled on December 2, 1953, and had a parole program requiring him to live with his mother in west Los Angeles. He stayed with his mother for approximately ten months and then "disappeared," taking his mother's car with him. Two days later he was captured hitchhiking near Kit Carson, Colorado. He was carrying a hunting knife and a ten-foot section of rope and was quoted as saying that he was returning "to kill my father."

Still, everyone in the corrections department continued to

---

* See memos at end of this story.

have hope and empathy for Jimmy. He was paroled a third time three years later but was again returned to prison for being arrested carrying a stolen revolver. Then, again in 1971, he was paroled but returned for passing bad checks.

Finally, the Bent County District Court set aside Jimmy's sentence, and he was to be released without conditions. When he was summoned to leave the prison, he hid under his bed and resisted all efforts to get him out. I was called to the cell block and pulled him from under the bed. He was incoherent and did not want to leave the prison even though his sentence had been completed. I sent him to Pueblo to the State Hospital, and that was the last that I ever heard of him until his death in Los Angeles ended the long trip of forty years.

Following is what I saw as the paradox of Roy Best. He was a consummate politician. He was adored by administrative and clerical employees at the State Capitol and took time to tell

Warden Roy Best (far right), Jimmy Melton (second from right)
as part of a posse.

jokes and visit with them when making an appearance in Denver.

He seemed to thrive on the publicity when an execution took place. He would invite large groups to witness the proceedings, and he personally took charge of carrying out all phases of the ceremony. During his time as warden, he conducted twenty-eight executions and was official witness at five others. Roy, with the condemned man in shackles and lead chains, would personally conduct the "last mile" to the gas chamber (on the hill behind the prison) – the "jornado del muerte" as the Hispanics called it. He had supported former Warden F. E. Crawford's statement that hanging was a brutal and inhumane method of carrying out the death penalty and had worked to have the law changed to the gas chamber.

Roy and I were friends, and I ignored his "other side" even though I was aware of his shortcomings. To me, he was a friendly, gregarious man. He didn't hesitate a moment in making me or his other friends the butt of some of his practical jokes, and he seemed to have an endless supply. He was a great teacher in the vagaries of human nature.

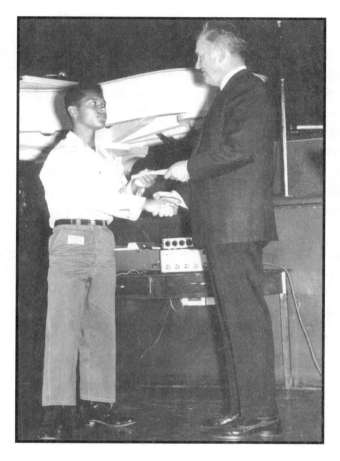

*Warden Patterson presenting a
GED Certificate to his youngest prisoner –
12 years old. Later the inmate was
transferred to Buena Vista.
During Patterson's administration,
he emphasized the importance of
education for the inmates.*

THE SPIDER MAN

For the whole world, without a native home,
is nothing but a prison of larger room.

-Cowley

On November 18, 1942, Theodore (#22813) entered the prison to start a life term. A small, scrawny man of fifty-two years, the intake officer reported that he had said, "Thank God! It's warm here and sounds like a noisy home." Theo, the wandering nomad, who for the most of forty-five years had slept in hobo jungle, boxcars, chicken houses, hay barns, city building air vents and, lastly, a foul attic, had at last found a home.

Like most prisoners, he quickly adapted to the regimented prison life and was required to take on some form of work. Attempting to assign Theo to a work station, Classification Officer Bob Manly asked if he had a trade. "No," Theo replied, adding, "but when I was living in that attic, I wired up a light by tapping into the electrical circuit." He was immediately sent to the electric shop where he labored for the next fifteen years and became quite expert in electrical repair. Theo was devoted to the electrical shop supervisor, Bill Davis, an old-time, hard-nosed prison officer, but also a thoughtful, caring man who belied the picture usually painted of hard, cold prison personnel.

Theo became eligible for parole in the mid 1950s, and I began a series of interviews with him for his appearance before the Parole Board. At that time he had the appearance of a polite, educated man. He had read almost every book in the prison library and could converse on many complicated subjects. The first interview was short as he advised me that he did not wish to be considered for parole. "I have no place to go, no outside friends, no relatives, and I wish to stay here." Thereafter, each year he routinely waived parole hearings, again emphasizing, "This is the only home I have ever known. I do not wish to leave here except on the gurney to the "Hill.""*

During the annual interviews, he gave me a coherent story of his strange journey through life. Theo was born in 1890 to an immigrant Ukranian mother and English father who worked as a shoemaker. His father was killed in a warehouse fire when he was five, leaving the mother and two sisters. With no income for the family, at age nine Theo began a life of wandering around the streets of Boston, New York and Philadelphia, carrying a ragged blanket and sleeping wherever night found him. He had a mandolin which he played on street corners, asking that handouts of money be dropped into a tin cup. At age twelve, he worked as a coal sorter in the Pennsylvania coal mines, migrating south with the advent of winter. While in Alabama, at age sixteen, he contracted tuberculosis and was carried from the streets near death. After his recovery, he was advised by the director of a street mission to move to Arizona. He traveled to Phoenix and made an attempt at panhandling but was so shy that he met with little success. Finally, a retired business man by the name of Peters (who lived in Denver, but spent time with a business he owned in Arizona) gave Theo a job cleaning offices.

However, Theo continued his nomadic existence and was arrested and jailed periodically. Finally, he faced the winter of 1941 in Denver and looked in the telephone book to try to locate his former patron, Mr. Peters. There were several individuals by

---

*Woodpecker Hill (see Glossary.)

the name of Peters listed, so Theo decided to go to the home of one and see if it were his former mentor.

Approaching a modest bungalow in north Denver, he knocked on the door but received no answer. As it was getting colder, he tried the door, found it unlocked and went inside. There he discovered a note written to a neighbor stating that the occupants (persons named Peters) would not return for several days and requesting the neighbor to check the home during their absence. Theo found ample food in the home, dined and proceeded to prowl about the house. He located in a bedroom closet an overhead door that led to a warm attic. Hearing a noise at the front door, he scrambled into the attic and, without determining whether he had found the Peters he sought, the "Spider Man" soon became ensconced in a cozy "web."

Phillip Peters, age seventy-three, and his wife were Theo's unwitting landlords for several months before his presence was discovered. Waiting until the elderly couple retired for the night, he would come down from the attic, secure a blanket, utensils, food and then return to his web. Occasionally, he would go down early in the morning before the Peters were awake. These early morning forays led to his crime, as Peters caught him in the act of raiding the cupboard. A struggle ensued, and Theo grabbed a stove lifter and beat the old man to death. Then, he retreated to his web!

Upon arising, Mrs. Peters found her husband lying on the kitchen floor and summoned the police. The police conducted a lengthy investigation; however, Mrs. Peters was of no help, and it seemed that, other than the stove lifter, nothing was disturbed in the house that gave any clues. Theo, of course, stayed in the attic during the investigation and only emerged at night after things quieted down. Mr. Peters was buried and Mrs. Peters and her "guest," now a murderer, continued to live in the bungalow for nearly a year.

At various times, Mrs. Peters heard odd noises in the house and once thought she heard the soft strumming of a guitar, but she attributed these incidents to a natural disquiet after the murder of her husband. Finally, she decided to move to another residence and thought she had left the house vacant. Not so! The Spider Man stayed on.

However, life for Theo had changed – no more refrigerator or cupboards of food, no warm furnace, no water. So he started to prowl around and burglarize the neighborhood. As the neighbors began to discover small thefts of food and clothing from their homes, they called the police and also reported weird sounds, music and "ghostly lights" in the empty house.

Unable to find anything amiss after looking through the empty home, the police decided to "stake out" the residence for a few nights. One policeman heard some noise and upon investigation saw Theo's feet disappearing into the attic door. The policeman followed and discovered a ragged, filthy and frightened man cowering in one corner. Upon searching further, the police found dirty blankets, papers, food scraps, empty food cans and a cardboard trough emptying into the gutter under the eaves which served as a toilet. An unbearable stench completed the picture. The Spider Man was a strange sight to the jailers when he was booked into jail, and his story was on the front pages of the Denver papers for a long period of time after his capture. The reporters labeled Theo the "Spider Man" and pictured him as darting out from his "web" in the attic to secure food and then hiding in the center of the web to eat. Mr. Peters was depicted as a "bee" that had to be killed to stop the web from being destroyed.

In 1964, Theo suffered a series of strokes which did not affect his mind but did affect his physical condition. Confined to a wheel chair he was consigned to a room in the hospital area of the prison that had been set aside for geriatrics. Officer Bill Davis visited him nearly every day at the hospital and brought him reading material and other needs until his death.

The Parole Board* once again offered to free Theo and arrange for his care in an outside nursing home; however, he politely (but firmly) declined, saying to me, "Warden, you wouldn't throw an old man out into the street, would you?"

Those of us who have homes and people who care for us probably can't empathize with a person who spent his entire life homeless and very much alone. During twenty-six years in the prison, Theo received no mail and no visitors. When tourists went through the prison,** three of the most often asked questions were, "Where is the Spider Man?" "Is he still alive?" and "How old is he now?" Little did they realize as they peered into the electrical shop during the tour that the little man working at the desk by the door was "The Spider Man."

---

*When Theo first became eligible for parole, I was the Director of Parole. He was still in prison when I became the warden. I visited the Geriatric Ward of the prison hospital about once a month and Theo was always quite talkative with me and the other elderly prisoners. He had a lot of time to educate himself, and he liked to test his knowledge with others.

**Tourists were taken on walking tours through the prison until after I retired in 1972. The prisoners protected the tours because they promoted the sale of the curios and paintings done by the inmates. Some 40,000 persons toured the prison during my last year as warden.

GOING FOR AN OSCAR

Live o'er each scene, and be what they behold.
- Pope, prologue to Addison's Cato

Doug was a budding Hollywood actor. Up to 1950 his roles had been mostly supporting ones; however, he was six feet four inches in height, handsome with a wavy shock of ash-blonde hair and had garnered a part with Burt Lancaster in the classic movie, *The Killers*. He lived in Hollywood and seemed destined for stardom. Then came a period of time when his agent could find no suitable roles for him. There seemed to be brighter days in the future but nothing in the present. Doug was faced with rent, food and entertainment bills and had pawned several items to pay his most urgent creditors.

Finally, a call came from his agent. He needed to provide an actor for a role that called for some travel but would only last three days and would pay five thousand, plus expenses. To thespian Doug it sounded like a windfall from heaven.

"What was the part?" Doug asked.

The agent explained that it had some minimal risks. The worst scenario was that Doug, or a still unknown partner, could be charged with fraud or confidence game if anything went wrong. The role – that of an armed security guard.

A meeting was held with the producer, a former Denver police officer named Singer. The story line was gone over in detail and sounded great. Doug decided that five grand would carry him over to his next role and agreed to play the part of security guard. He *would be* involved in a crime, but it appeared "fool proof" with no chance of getting caught.

On the day that the action was to begin, Doug entered the business offices on the top floor of the Daniels & Fisher Tower in downtown Denver. Dressed in a security guard's uniform of light blue shirt, tan pants with a black strip down the leg and a .38 caliber gun in the holster of his Sam Browne belt, Doug arrived at exactly 8:50 a.m. and entered the dual elevator doors on the south side of the offices. Behind a waist-high counter, he could see several secretaries chatting as they made coffee. Bantering with the secretaries, he waited patiently while a large safe was opened. One of the women handed him a canvas bag containing the previous day's receipts, and at 8:55 a.m. Doug went down in the elevator.

Then, at 9:00 a.m. the elevator doors reopened, and a security guard entered the room to collect yesterday's receipts for the armored car waiting in the street below. At first, the secretaries did not seem to understand that this guard was not Doug and thought he must have forgotten something. When the second guard finally was able to convince the women that he had not been in the tower earlier, great confusion ensued as the store manager and the police were called.

While all of the above was occurring, Doug had gotten into a rented car and headed for a rendezvous somewhere east of Denver with the former police officer. He removed his Sam Browne belt, cut it into pieces and threw the pieces out of the car and into the barrow pit. Turning onto a side road, he parked the car, climbed a fence into a cornfield already heavy with the fall harvest and traveled about a half mile up the rows of corn. There he dug a hole, deposited the pistol and covered it with dirt. Then he placed his uniform and cap in a pile, opened the cash bag and dumped all of the checks on top of his clothing and set everything on fire.

Unfortunately, Doug didn't hang around until everything was completely burned as he figured that nothing would remain from the fire, and he had committed the perfect crime. Never contemplating that he had left clues in the cornfield that would lead to all three robbers, Doug hiked out of the cornfield and got back in his auto with, as near as he could count, about $50,000. He met the ex-policeman at Byers, Colorado, and they both returned to California and turned the money over to the conspirators. Doug collected his $5,000, paid his debts and waited for the "big role" to come his way.

Unknown to Doug when he was burning evidence was that the farmer who owned the cornfield was mending harness behind his barn about two miles from the site of Doug's fire. When the farmer saw a little wisp of smoke in his field, he thought some pheasant hunter might have tossed away a cigarette. Cursing the hunter, he got on his saddle horse and went to investigate. When the farmer found the little pile of partially burned checks and clothing, he promptly called the sheriff. The "perfect crime" began to unravel.

The signed checks were traced to Daniels & Fisher, and, with a little digging, the gun was recovered and traced to ex-provisional Denver policeman Singer[*] who was then living in California. Singer and Doug's agent began to talk and talk and talk. They placed all of the blame on Doug, and then he also began to talk. The result was that Doug was arrested and returned to Denver for trial. The agent was extradited to Colorado from California for trial, even though he contended that he had never been in Colorado so it was impossible for him to be convicted of a crime in that state. (He was acquitted.) The policeman had a terminal illness and died.

---

[*] An April 30, 1998, article in *The Denver Post* cited a 1984 historical item as follows: "A 39-year-old provisional policeman admitted engineering the sensational 'armed guard' robbery of the Daniels and Fisher department store, Denver police officials said."

Doug's role in the robbery may have rated "Oscar" consideration, but hurried bungling negated the great acting. "Leading man" Doug spent the next few years reading movie magazines in a 5' x 7' cell at night and making license plates by day.

I interviewed Doug when he became eligible for parole and secured a job for him as a car salesman at a Denver dealership. He served the balance of his sentence in Colorado and appeared in television commercials every day, hawking automobiles. Doug turned out to be a natural salesman and may have been the early-day prototype of salesmen appearing in later commercials. He sold cars to prison officers he knew from the prison, and the dealer said he sold more cars than the other salesmen combined. His parole agent also mentioned that Doug was always surrounded by a bevy of good looking women.

For several years after he returned to California, Doug corresponded with his assigned parole agent and with me – but no acting was forthcoming and no Oscars!

"SOFT SHOE" BRYANT
– ROBIN HOOD OF THE 1950s

Skilled in every trick,
He could make black look white and white look black.
- Ovid

Part of my on-the-job training as a public official came during my time as Executive Director of the State Department of Parole (1951-1957). The parole agents and I, with some law enforcement and social work experience behind us, presumed ourselves to be rather worldly and "con wise" when it came to supervising parolees. We soon discovered that the marker between naiveté and gullibility was very narrow when we were required to supervise "well-calcified" confidence men. "Soft Shoe" was an outstanding example of a veteran con man, teaching us neophytes the art of carrying out some daring and profitable business practices that posed a minimal risk of discovery. We, of course, had to learn too late!

Soft Shoe rented and lived in a small house near Rocky Flats. Daily he commuted to Stapleton Airport where he had a job as a Redcap and a part-time job at the shoeshine stand. He was about sixty years old, short and pudgy with a fringe of gray hair at the temples, friendly and outgoing and a consummate entertainer, particularly at the shine stand. He would blow on a small mouth harp while shining shoes, snapping the shine cloth in rhythm as he sang, whistled and danced. Since he was well-known to the airport travelers, he usually attracted a crowd to the shine stand.

Earlier in his life, Soft Shoe had been a Pullman Porter on the railroad. It was on this job that he developed an extra avocation that caused his arrest and conviction for a crime known then as "Confidence Game." In dealing with "the suckers" Soft Shoe did not rely on only one modus operandi but utilized several types of scams.

A sly fox, Soft Shoe knew from his railroad job shortly after World War II that there was a shortage of good liquor in Denver. During his time off he would read both Denver newspapers thoroughly and would note where businessmen were to be out of town for several days at a convention or business meetings. After calling the office of the businessman to make certain the man was away, Soft Shoe would don his old Pullman Porter's uniform and carrying a box labeled "Canadian Scotch Whiskey" go to the victim's office suite, place the box on the secretary's desk and ask for the businessman by his first name.

"Ma'am, is Mr. Jack here?" When told that the man in question was out of town for a few days, he would ask, "What can I do with this stuff that was ordered by Mr. Jack?"

The secretary, at a loss as to what to do, would have Soft Shoe take the "stuff" into the boss's closet and would pay the bill – usually $125 – in cash. When the boss returned and was told by the secretary about the delivery, the box would be opened only to show that it contained either quart jars filled with water or about twenty-five cents worth of sprouting potatoes and a small bottle of water – to provide sound.

The secretary could be of little help except to remember that the perpetrator wore a uniform and she thought it was a black man with gray hair. Telephoning other business colleagues who had been out of town at the same meeting, the businessman would learn that the same thing had happened to their secretaries who also could not provide a description of the culprit. When the police were called in to investigate, no trace of the con-man in uniform could be found. Their investigation revealed many other incidents of the same type of fraud, but none of the businessmen wanted their names connected to the crimes, especially if there were to be embarrassing publicity in the local newspapers.

The police also noted some new fraud complaints which appeared to be by a man fitting the description of the one who had delivered the "phony" scotch. It was Soft Shoe with a different *modus operandi*! With a mule and cart, Soft Shoe would wander through alleys and to landfills, gathering pieces of metal or scrap iron. Then, he would fill several barrels with rocks, top off the barrels with valuable looking scrap metal, spend weekends hauling the barrels to different metal dealers and collect dollars for the weight in "scrap". The dealers assumed they were getting some great bargains until they dumped the barrels. Meanwhile Soft Shoe was becoming wealthy. One metal dealer called the police but could not describe the man who sold him the "rocks" except that he was black and had gray hair.

Several months later the metal dealer was at the airport and while awaiting departure time, he wandered over to where a crowd was being entertained by a shoe shine man. The metal dealer did a "double take" when he saw the entertainer and decided he had found the "rock" salesman. The police were called and Soft Shoe was taken into custody. His past record was checked; he was convicted of Confidence Game and was given twelve to twenty years in prison.

Soft Shoe was assigned to the Officers' Barber Shop in the prison where I first met him. He continued his entertaining ways – singing, dancing and playing the mouth harp accompanied by the rhythmic snapping of the shining cloth as he buffed shoes. While working in the prison barber shop he collected many tips and had a nice nest egg when he was released on parole on September 19, 1952, and, interestingly enough, he got his old job at the airport shoe stand.

However, serving time in prison apparently had not dampened Soft Shoe's need to be a con man. The temptation of dealing with more suckers was too much for him to pass up, and he moved on to yet another *modus operandi*.

One morning he appeared at the Parole office grief stricken. He advised the Parole Officer that he had just been told that his mother was terminally ill at the family home in Oklahoma and requested permission to travel there to visit his dying mother. The request was immediately granted with no investigation. Over several months Soft Shoe made regular trips to see his ill mother and after each trip reported her fading health. Then one morning Parole Officer Charlie Simmons received a call from a Sheriff in Oklahoma. Charlie, an African American, talked to the sheriff for a few seconds and then quickly handed the phone to me.

"Offisuh, we got a Nigga by the name a Bryant down heah bootleggin'. You know Oklahoma is drah, and he's bringin' some watted down Colorado whiskey in heah and bootleggin' it to everybody." Then the Sheriff chuckled and said, "He's sellin' it to evah banka, lawya and business man in the county, at ten bucks a pint. It's about ten pacent whiskey, a spoon of brown suga' and the rest watta'. All his customas tell me that the byin' is done by someone else – not them – so ah can't do anythin' about it unless ah ketch him redhanded. So if he's on parole in Colorado, ah'd sure appreciate it if you would relieve me of his presence in ma county."

We explained to the Sheriff that he was in Oklahoma to visit his dying mother. The Sheriff laughed again and said, "His mamma ain't dyin'. She's in good health, and I see her nearly evah day. She's a nice haad working lady, and she's raised some good kids – except thisson."

We told the Sheriff to jail Soft Shoe, who, we later learned, had purchased (with cash) a used but flashy Cadillac. Soft Shoe was brought back from Oklahoma and we had decided to suspend his parole when we received a call from a Colonel in the Salvation Army in Denver. The Colonel stated that Soft Shoe had been a heavy and faithful contributor for several years, and he hoped that we wouldn't be hasty in revoking his parole. The Colonel further added that he would volunteer to appear before the Parole Board on Bryant's behalf, if it were permissible.

Since we were surprised at this information, we decided to investigate further. We found that Soft Shoe did not regularly attend church but had financially contributed to two churches and was well known to the pastors, favorably. He never, as far as we could determine, victimized any poor or elderly individuals – only wealthy white men. The white men that we interviewed denied being victimized and were of no help; however, we did advise them that the "confidence money," or at least some of it, had gone to good causes.

We continued Soft Shoe's parole, but his reputation with the Parole Board as a modern Robin Hood left the Parole Officer with no tools of control except to threaten dire consequences if he continued his tricks.

These incidents occurred forty years ago, but if Soft Shoe is still alive, he will be looking for the wealthy suckers. If he has passed on, he will be laughing, singing and dancing with the gods – and he will probably sell something "up there" if the right, gullible angel should happen along.

Warden Patterson talking with
condemned inmate Sylvester Garrison.
See story, "The Power of Positive thinking."

BETTER THAN THE LOTTERY

There is no witness so dreadful,
no accuser so terrible as the conscience
that dwells in the heart of every man.
-Polybius

In the small western town dusk had fallen as Alfred made his way down the dusty alley. He stopped and cautiously peered over the fence at a small white house. A burglar, thief, escape artists and sometimes a stickup, Alfred had led several prisoners on an escape from the old Larimer County jail in Fort Collins; but soon abandoned his partners and drifted to California and then to New Mexico. Eventually, he landed back in Colorado where he was employed, mostly for his board and room, at menial tasks in various small-town restaurants. After a short period of this unrewarding existence, he again took up his former career of burglarizing homes.

Although a pink glow still tinged the clouds overhead, lights shone from the windows of nearby houses and the odor of frying meat filled the late summer air. However, no lights were visible in the house he was watching and he could see that the back door was ajar. Apparently no one was home and the owners had forgotten to lock the back door. This looked like a safe prospect to rob.

Quietly he opened the wooden gate and moved quickly across the yard, pausing to listen by the open door. No sounds came from inside the dark home. Opening the door, Alfred crept onto a small porch and then made his way into the kitchen. As he reached the door of the living room, the silence was broken as a soft voice asked, "Is that you, son?"

Alfred was stunned. Peering across the room in the faint light, he could just see an elderly woman seated in a rocker near a window. Finally, he got up the nerve to say just one word, "Yep." He had gone too far to retreat so he moved closer to the woman and blurted, "I need some money."

The old woman continued to slowly rock in her chair and responded, "You know where the money is, son. Take what you need and get the grocery list you made out and bring them when you come back."

The word "money" rang in Alfred's ears. He had entered the home to burglarize it, not expecting to find anyone home. The woman was staring at him and yet for some reason she still thought he was her son. Finally, it dawned on Alfred. The old woman was blind!

Alfred's mind began to work. He did not know where the money was. How could he find out without the old lady sensing that he was not the person she thought he was? After a moment of silence, Alfred gambled. "Mom, you've changed the place, haven't you?"

"No," she replied. "It's still on the top shelf."

Immediately, Alfred removed his shoes to keep noise at a minimum and began to prowl around the house, giving particular attention to top shelves. His luck held and on the top shelf of a bedroom closet he found the money – two shoe boxes crammed with bills. Alfred had won the lottery with a blind lady calling the numbers.

Gambling that the old woman still thought he was her son, Alfred returned to the living room and said, "Mom, I'll be back as soon as I get the groceries."

"Fine," came the woman's reply. "Be sure to leave a light on in the kitchen, son, because it will be dark when you get back."

Replacing his shoes, Alfred scurried out the back door and down the alley where he had parked his car. Arriving at the run-down boarding house where he was in arrears with his rent, he quickly switched on the light, pulled the shades and began to count the money. The first box contained $25,556, and Alfred's hands shook as he searched for a pencil and scrap of paper on which to write down the numbers. The second box was of a more ancient vintage and contained many large "Horse Blanket" bills. As he counted and stacked $24,590 dollars in bills on the swaybacked bed, his breathing became shallow, and he could feel sweat break out on his forehead. By now his fourth grade education was sorely tested as he added the contents of the two boxes together. The final tally – $50,146.

Now Alfred had some new decisions to face. He could not remain in the small town and use much of the money as people would question his sudden affluence. Where could he go? Las Vegas? New York? With this much money he could fly to Brazil. Joe, the con man with whom he had escaped from jail, had said that a person could not be extradited from Brazil.

While Alfred was pondering his next move, the old woman's son arrived home and learned what had occurred earlier. After repeatedly denying that he had taken any money, the son finally called the sheriff. It would later be determined that neither the son nor the mother knew the exact amount of money in the shoe boxes as it had been stashed away by the father before his death. The mother thought it was just a modest amount, and the son knew only that mom replenished her purse from time to time from a cache somewhere in the house. The mother refused to cooperate with the sheriff, as she was positive that the son had taken the money. Alfred was home free without even the IRS in on the windfall.

Sketchy details of Alfred's story were first related to me by the sheriff from Walsenburg who brought him to the prison. Later Alfred filled out the story as related above. Although he had not been bothered with much sign of a conscience during his earlier crime-spotted life, he had qualms about stealing from the trusting blind lady and thought of his own mother. Stealing the life savings from a blind woman was too much for even this hardened criminal's conscience.

Women
In Prison

WOMEN IN THE PRISON

There is no worse evil than a bad woman; and nothing
has ever been produced better than a good one.
-Euripides

During my stewardship of Colorado's two penal institutions there were few women confined in the women's section. In 1950 there were 35 females in the prison, and that number varied little until the late 1960s when more females began to be sentenced on drug-related charges, embezzlement, bad check writing and other minor, non-violent crimes. The prison in Cañon City was also contracting for female prisoners from the adjoining states – Utah, South Dakota, New Mexico and Wyoming. Generally, courts in the U.S. were reluctant to sentence women to prison, except for very serious offenses or continuous violent or aggressive types of crimes. By the 1960s, however, the profile of women in prison was one of mostly very tough women.

The rate of women in prison continued to grow rapidly until the 1982 Federal Bureau of Prison statistics indicated the rate was 150% more than males. One reason seemed to be that women were growing rapidly in the work force and had more opportunity to commit white collar crimes. Also, district attorneys and judges had become less lenient and more willing to prosecute female offenders.

At Vienna, Illinois, penal administrators established a large coeducational institution in an attempt to absorb women into constructive programs provided for males. The effort was not

93

very successful, as I recall. Housing for the sexes was at opposite ends of a college-type campus, with programs in the central area. The architecture was perfect, but the penologists were only dreaming. Friction developed when women were allowed to wear civilian clothing, and the males were required to wear prison garb. The rules also stated no touching or contact between sexes although they dined in the same room. As time went on, the enforcement of these rules required double the number of staff for the endless and nonproductive surveillance. Warden Vern Housewright in Illinois told me that the coed system had one plus: "Men are combing their hair, using cologne and showering more often."

Officers at the Women's Correctional Facility built in the late 1960s.

The practice of housing men and women within the same institution had been the "norm" in Colorado; however, it was decided that the sexes should be separated, and in 1966 plans were drawn for a new women's facility to be set away from the shadow of the old prison walls. The plan, after completion of the new prison, was to change the classification of female personnel to "officers" instead of the historic title of "matron" and train the new staff accordingly. May Gillespie was appointed Associate

Warden with one assistant, two sergeants and twenty staff officers – all female* – who would supervise ninety female prisoners. At that time the only male at the women's prison was the maintenance man.

The institution would provide a large number of new programs, including: vocational training in clerical, typing and office work, food service, hair styling and makeup (a three-chair beauty shop), janitorial and domestic services, and sewing (which would later be converted to industrial-type clothing production). Qualified teachers were employed to provide basic

Women in dresses they had made in sewing class.

---

* Women who worked in the men's prison were only allowed to work outside of the security perimeter, mostly in clerical or secretarial positions. Later, with the advent of the equal treatment laws and with some heavy nudging from the federal courts, women were placed in positions in the towers. The main limitation to the positions for women was that no female was to work in any area of the male prison where dressing or undressing took place, and the same limitation applied to males working in the female areas. Also, females were never to be without escorts in the male prison – except on the towers.

reading, writing and math instruction with a goal of having inmates qualify for their GED. In addition, the institution had a large recreation area, chapel, library, modern kitchen and dining area, outside exercise yard with softball field and basketball court and, instead of cells, attractive rooms.

Vocational Program graduates at the new female unit.
May Gillespie, Associate Warden, is in the center of the group.

I assumed that the women inmates would be delighted with the change from the old, crowded prison they had left behind. But NO! Two weeks later two young girls climbed over the outside fence and escaped.* Then, one month after the move to the new facility I was returning from Denver when my radio "came alive." The women were rioting at the new prison! May

---

* They had done no planning, only that one had a boyfriend who, supposedly, was going to pick them up. Instead, they thumbed a ride from an individual who turned out to be a prison officer searching for them. They were tired and hungry and told Warden Gillespie that they were glad to get caught.

Gillespie said the riot developed after a fight between two women, and then everyone became involved in the disturbance. The women threw a lot of missiles and broke a couple of windows, but mostly the melee consisted of screaming, hair pulling, cursing and fighting among themselves. One girl was cut on the arm by a pair of scissors. Who were the instigators of this turmoil? As usual, two of my most troublesome prisoners, Yvette and Sylvia.*

---

* See following story.

"I don't like this reform. Now, when something's wrong, instead of yelling 'GUARD'—we have to call out 'CORRECTIONAL OFFICER'!"

Cartoon from the Cor-Em News,
a publication of the Colorado State Penitentiary.
January 1972 (page 9)

YVETTE *VS.* SYLVIA

*These two hated each other with a hate
found only on the stage.*

-Byron

I had always been a fight fan. I listened on the radio to the two Jack Dempsey and Gene Tunney fights. I was rooting for Dempsey because I had seen him when he was living and fighting in Montrose, and he was a ranch hand for a short time at our neighbor's ranch nearby.* After moving to Denver I was a fan of Joe Louis, George Manley and Muhammad Ali. However, never did I imagine I would become a referee or boxing commissioner. When I became Warden of the prison, suddenly I became both! My involuntary appointment came as I was forced to referee a series of battles between two very tough "ladies."

Yvette was a black woman from Texas who had been convicted and sentenced in Denver. Too small to be a welterweight (maybe a lightweight), she became a heavyweight when fight time came. Sylvia was another beauty, a native American, who was about the same weight as Yvette but a half a head taller. She came from Southern Colorado, and she must have inherited some of Crazy Horse's genes, because she was a real warrior when fight time came.

Whenever the two began to fight, there was no screaming,

---

* I spent my early years on a ranch west of Montrose.

hair pulling or scratching. They boxed – jabbing, feinting, thrusting, clinching while all the time using fancy footwork. Punching at each other with their fists, they could make the Marquis of Queensberry look like a brawler and Muhammad Ali look like a rank amateur. They also used words that described heritage in terms I'd never heard in my 30 years of work with the "devil's disciples." They would fight to a standstill, cursing and struggling with the matrons and other officers who were trying to halt the match.

Since I viewed this type of female behavior as unseemly and disruptive to the peace and quiet of the institution, I ordered the women placed in a "quiet cell" next to each other where they had to sit and sleep on a concrete bed for several days.[*] The cell was wired into the office of May Gillespie, the Associate Warden at the Women's Prison, to allow us to determine when their behavior had become modified enough to be acceptable to themselves and other prisoners. Needless to say, one day a rather unflattering comment about the Warden was heard. "That old son-of-a-bitch will keep us here forever. We've got to promise him no more fighting."

About the third day the two women would ask to see me and swear that they would never fight again if they could only get off the concrete bunks. I would give them a free lecture and another day to solidify their thinking and also remind them that I didn't care for their use of foul language. Then I would order their release and return to my duties at the relatively quiet male section, a completely separate institution housing over 1,600 prisoners compared with the noisy female institution of 35 women. However, my peace was usually short lived.

"Warden," my Associate Warden May Gillespie would say in a resigned voice, "Sylvia and Yvette are at it again, and

---

[*] Male prisoners were put on a diet of bread and spinach; however, the females were given regular meals unless they threw their food back at the officers.

they have the whole institution stirred up. I simply don't know what to do with them."

Over time, all of us, Sylvia and Yvette included, developed a liking for each other, and the incidents became a kind of a repetitious game – war and then a short peace and another war. I think the women fought just to get me to come over to the women's unit as it probably made for an interesting diversion in the otherwise boring prison routine.

Often May and I would laugh at the fights and the aftermath, as long as no one was seriously injured. We both learned that we were several types of SOBs and that we were "born of unwedded parents." Still, we didn't take the slurs personally as it was all in a day's work – and I did get to become a qualified fight referee! May Gillespie also became a referee while the other women prisoners became fans and managers of

Yvette receives her School Achievement Certificate from Warden Patterson.

the two sparring women as the scenario was constantly repeated. What they fought about I never knew.

Sylvia was married to a convict for a period of time and only made one more trip to the prison. However, in 1969, I had occasion to tour the Texas prison system with its director, Dr. George Beto. When we visited the women's prison, several miles outside Huntsville, the female warden at this institution said to Dr. Beto, "There is a girl in dormitory "D" who wishes to speak to Warden Patterson." (Obviously, the prison grapevine was at work.)

I said, "Sure," and we sat down in the dining room to wait. Who showed up? Yvette and her sister Martha. Dr. Beto and the warden, who were sitting at the table with us, laughed as Yvette told the story of her "doing time" in Colorado.

FATHER OF THE BRIDE

The bride hath paced into the hall,
Red as a rose is she.

Coleridge

Sometimes nice things happen when you have oversight of eighty female offenders. Such was the case in 1968 when a little Hispanic girl arrived at the prison. Tina was several months pregnant and unable to identify the father, although she had a boyfriend. According to her story, she had attended a party, had taken too many drinks and had gone into a bedroom in the house to lie down. She awoke sometime later in the darkened room, nearly nude, to discover a man dressing himself. Because the room was dark, she was unable to identify the man. Eventually, police arrived and the partygoers (including Tina) were arrested and convicted of a drug charge. Tina stated to Associate Warden May Gillespie that she and her boyfriend Enrique had been indulging in sexual activities for some time, and she was hopeful that he was the father.

Prior to the birth of the baby, Tina asked permission to marry Enrique. She had a host of supporters among the other prisoners who begged May to give Tina a "full scale" wedding ceremony. May conferred with me, and we both conferred with Father Justin. Soon, staff, prisoners, Enrique and several relatives of the bride and groom became involved in planning the nuptials.

Father Justin insisted that there must be a "father of the

103

bride." But there was none as Tina's father was dead. Fr. Justin just grinned at me and said," Warden, it's either you or the maintenance man."

So, I decided to become father of the bride. I put on my best pinstripe suit, and Tina dressed in a white wedding dress and veil which had been made by the women in the sewing unit. She took my arm and we moved slowly into the chapel to the tune of a Mexican wedding march played on the organ. Fr. Justin droned on with the wedding ceremony in Latin, I gave the bride away to Enrique, and a happy reception followed.

Unlike many prison stories, this one had a happy ending. Tina gave birth to a healthy baby, and subsequent blood tests determined that Enrique was the father. Enrique's mother kept the baby for a few months until Tina was released.

I had several notes and cards from Tina after her release, and she wrote often to May Gillespie. Enrique and Tina seemed to "live happily ever after."

THE KEEPER
BECOMES "GHOST-BUSTER"

So many ghosts, and forms of fright
Have started from their graves tonight.
-Longfellow

The old warden's residence at Buena Vista was a classic place to live for anyone interested in ethology of ghostly apparitions. Built in the late 1880s as a barracks for officers, originally it had twelve upstairs bedrooms with a long stairway leading from ground level to the center six rooms. The residence had been remodeled* several times – the last with the warden and family occupying the front upstairs rooms and the back six rooms locked, except when guests or state officers were entertained.

The first night I stayed alone at the residence as I had left my wife Mary in Denver to prepare for our move. As I turned out the lights and climbed the stairs, I heard someone run up the stairs behind me. I turned, but there was no one there. During the night there were seemingly endless noises – people talking, someone running up and down the stairs, something banging on the side of the house. Lights would come on in locked back rooms which had been dark when I first checked them. In any event, I did not believe

---

* My family and I were the last to live in the old residence as it was razed in 1962 and a new residence constructed. I had been appointed Warden in 1957 but did not assume all duties until the previous warden had used his vacation time.

in ghosts, so I spent most of the next several nights attempting to discover the cause of the mysterious events. I found that the loudest banging noise was the steam heating system expanding and contracting as it came from the boiler house. Unlike me, Mary and our daughter Tammy took a long time to adjust to the eerie sounds. Many of our guests spoke of strange sights and sounds after they had spent the night in the extra bedrooms.

About that same time we were given a German police puppy which we named Joe T. He slept at the head of the stairs, and one night he started barking. I got up to see what had disturbed him and found him looking at one of the doors to the locked rooms, hair on his back raised. When I finally got the door opened, Joe T. rushed past me and stood barking at the bare wall of the room. I

Fran in cell #18
with one of her parakeets.

could see nothing there, but, apparently, he did. Gradually he ceased barking and moved away from the wall. (I have to admit that it was a bit spooky.)

Problems about ghosts also erupted at the women's prison.* One morning, May Gillespie called me and said, "I wish you would come over and talk to Edna. She seems to be losing her mind, and we may have to send her off to the State Hospital."

---

* This refers to the "old" women's prison outside the walls, which is now the Prison Museum. Prior to that facility being built, women were interned within the walls.

I met with May and an agitated Edna that afternoon. "Fran's in there talking to that bird in the middle of the night," Edna began, staring intently at me. "The bird chirps back, and then she moves her chair and furniture around. Pearl says #18 was her cell in the other building inside the walls, but she's been gone thirty years." Edna took a moment to get her breath and then continued. "I call the night matron, and she tells me, 'You know there is noboby in cell #18, so you shut up and get to sleep or you're going downstairs.' So I shut up, but I'm scared. Fran was here for killing a policeman."*

I asked Edna what cell she was in, and she said #17. "But Fran is still there in #18. None of the other women will stay in that cell for a minute, and Ms. Gillespie knows it."

I asked who was in cell #19, and May indicated it was a woman named Nellie. We talked with Nellie and after a bit of prodding, she agreed with Edna. "I hear sounds in the night that someone in that cell makes," she said in a fairly low voice, as if afraid there were someone else listening to her words. "There are strange noises, furniture moving and someone talking to one of those parakeet birds. I don't pay no attention. I get to sleep. I don't believe in ghosts, but Edna is right. A lot of strange sounds in the night in that cell."

May solved the problem by getting a newly sentenced, tough woman to live in cell #18. However, even after the women were moved to the new women's prison, there were constant rumors that ghosts occupied several areas of that building. One story was that Pearl had stabbed a woman in the doorway to the kitchen, and the bloodstain continued to appear even after extensive scrubbing.

---

* Fran had been a nurse at Denver General Hospital in 1929 or 1930. She had killed her longtime lover Evans, a Denver policeman, while he was a patient in that hospital. Originally, Fran had been confined in the old female prison (inside the walls) and had only lived in the women's prison outside the walls for a short time when she was paroled and later pardoned. For years there was constant gossip among the women about the haunting of the facility.

After the women had been to the present-day facility, I went over to the old building about 9:00 P.M. for the purpose of trying to determine a subsequent use for the facility. As I toured the building, I heard such a plethora of noises: steam lines banging, the walls cracking and popping, lights coming on before I hit a switch. There were sounds like women's voices and furniture being moved across the floor in part of the tier. I was glad to get out and go home.

The last job I had as a "ghostbuster" was with the "curse" that had been placed on cell #14 on condemned row. Luis Monge* was assigned cell #4 with John Bell in #3 and Joe Segura in #5. Apparently, Monge talked to someone or to himself at night. Bell told me the persons Monge talked with were named Silliman and Sonny. Bell said that he never saw anyone, but he did hear them walk late at night. "Sonny," Bell related, "yelled out that he and Silliman had put a curse on the 'row,' and it would remain forever."

I talked with the other prisoners on condemned row, but they just laughed. Garrison said, "We sure got ghosts, but they are kept *outside* our cells." He acted as if he were part of some joke. Monge refused to discuss the subject.

Later, on another trip that I made to condemned row, I noted Bell was still on the subject of "the curse" by Silliman and Sonny. I took a little time to look up the history of previous condemned men. Silliman and Howard "Sonny" Potts were on the row awaiting execution at the same time, in 1945. Silliman's wife, whom he had murdered, was a seer who claimed some ability to confer with the dead.

I closed the book and gave up on ghosts. However, a short time ago I talked with a Prison Museum worker who had seen bloodstains and heard furniture moving. She (the volunteer) knew nothing of all the previous haunting. However, I suspect the ghost tales will continue.

* See story titled "My Mamma."

Escapes
(or Attempts)

THE FROGMAN

Assume nothing as you labor in prisons
and only one-half of what you see and hear.
-WKP

This is the story of a young prisoner using "frogman" tactics, swimming under water with a snorkel for seventy-five yards, sawing through two-inch bars and nearly through the third before being forced to abort the escape attempt after losing his snorkel tube.

To set the stage for those readers who are not familiar with the prison grounds, there is a large waterway* which has been the site of several escapes and attempts to escape throughout the history of the prison. The canal is about fifteen feet wide and varies in depth, usually three and a half to four feet. It enters the prison from the west, flows under the arched, barred passageway under the wall beside the west gate tower into the prison grounds, curves slightly as it flows between the large cellblocks along an internal wall, exits the prison under the east wall and then proceeds through the city. Under each of the prison walls are two rows of upright steel bars about two inches in diameter, which must be breeched in order to effect an escape.

---

* This is an old irrigation canal, named the Hydraulic Irrigation Canal, that originally flowed by the front of the prison buildings but later was enclosed within the walls as the prison grounds expanded. In addition to escape attempts, the canal also served as a funnel for attempts to float contraband into the institution by innovative prisoners with outside contacts.

Canal which flows through prison with Tower 8 in the background.

The story begins with the arrival of Jimmy, a fifteen-year-old sturdily built, baby-faced youth sentenced to serve a life sentence for the murders of his father and mother. Jimmy appeared before the Classification Committee of the prison and was given the usual rules to govern his confinement. Then, for his protection, he was given some more specific instructions by the captain in charge of the Intake Unit, Captain Freddie Roche.

"Jimmy, we are going to give you a cell upstairs, and your work assignment will be janitorial work in this building. You are not to leave, except for meals, without the consent of the cell house officer. The reason for these precautions is because there are several prisoners here who would make you into a girl if you got into the wrong place or out of sight of the officers or towers. Do you understand?"

"Yes, sir," Jimmy replied meekly.

"Do you have a hobby or something you like to do in your spare time?"

"Yes, sir. I like to read, and I'd like to do leather work, but I have no money. My grandpa will send me some money for supplies if you allow me to do leather work."

Captain Roche nodded. "It's okay. Tell your grandpa to send you the money, and you see the officer in charge of the 'junk work,'* and he'll get the materials for you. Now, remember, stay where you can be seen if you are out of this area – for any reason."

Jimmy followed the rules, stayed in his cell when he wasn't working and kept a low profile. His grandmother and grandfather (parents of his murdered mother) visited him at times and provided money for the leather work. He read extensively – particularly a book about Navy frogmen and their equipment and their heroics as divers – but, as was discovered later, did little leather work. However, he did make good, if illegal, use of the shoe dyes and other materials provided for making leather objects. For a youth, he demonstrated remarkable patience as he planned and nearly carried out an amazing escape.

Jimmy's cell was one level above the pavement outside the building and about twenty steps from the canal. From the window in his cell, he could see the officer on tower eight who had oversight of the inside of the prison grounds. The prison at night was usually extremely quiet; cell lights were out and the only activity was the movement of the ground officers (those patrolling at ground level) making their rounds. A flood light from the towers flashed on as movement was detected, but a wave of the hand from the ground officer to the tower officer would get the flood light extinguished.

Over many months, Jimmy observed the night time activities of the tower eight officer and recorded the time of each routine activity that the officer made during each shift. He discovered that at exactly 11:00 p.m. the officer went to the far side of the tower to open a gate for the ground officer to go from the main grounds into the hospital area. This would set the time for Jimmy to drop from his cell window and into the canal – unseen.

---

* The term "junk work" applied to hobby work permitted to be done in the cells of trusty prisoners and then sold in the Prison Curio Shop.

Finally, Jimmy was ready. From a pair of long winter underwear he had made a suit and head hood and, using the dye provided for his leather work, had colored these and his shoes black. The "frogman" diving suit which would let him blend into the darkness was now complete. Jimmy gathered his equipment that had been accumulated and hidden over a long period of time (a hacksaw and several blades, a snorkle tube made from a piece of electrical conduit and wrapped in black tape, a pair of leather gloves dyed black, a plastic bag containing numerous small personal items) and sawed through the bars on his window. His fantasy of escape was about to become reality!

At 11:00 p.m., as the officer in tower eight was on the side away from his cell, Jimmy dropped out the window, jumped into the canal and with the snorkel in his mouth submerged into the

"Frogman" suit and hood, with related paraphenalia on table.

murky water. However, the current in the canal was stiffer than he had anticipated, and he had to struggle to get to the bars under the wall at the west gate. Finally reaching the bars, he began the laborious task of sawing through them. One bar, top and bottom gave way. Then he began to saw on the second bar. He knew if he could stay submerged long enough, he could cut a large hole, squeeze through and be free.

In the meantime, unaware of the activity near his feet, the ground officer was distributing the mid-shift meal to the officers in the towers. He approached the west gate tower only about ten feet from the frogman who was busy in the canal, sawing the final bar. Then, fate intervened. Fighting the heavy current, somehow the frogman lost his snorkel and had to surface.

For the night ground officer, his shift had been extremely quiet and, as usual, routinely boring. He was placing the lunch box on the rope* dangling from tower eight when suddenly a strange black creature with a round white face loomed out of the dark water – right at his feet! "It was the damnest, most shocking sight I ever saw," the officer explained later with a grin. "A heart attack was almost in the picture."

Frogman Jimmy was escorted back to a cell, and the later reassessment of the escape attempt showed that officers were collectively negligent in their duty in assuming that the sixteen-year-old inmate was incapable of carrying out a simple escape plot. No one had bothered to search Jimmy's cell as they had ASSUMED that he was a "kid" without any ability to connive let alone attempt to put together a complicated escape plan. The ground officer was given a few days off to recover from the unexpected experience of the "creature from the canal," and the entire episode was used for officers' training for several years. The officers involved in the incident learned that ASSUME is a dangerous word when used to guess at a fact in prison, and they

---

* A rope was dropped from the towers so that the officers in the tower could haul the attached meal up to their work station.

later adopted a type of slogan: ASSUME means ASS
__YOU__ME!!

After the escape attempt Jimmy was assigned to the general prison population and worked and lived in the hospital area. He became interested in becoming a medical technician and studied extensively for the next few years. He also developed athletically and participated in all of the prison sports activities.

Federal Judge John Kane[*] became interested in Jimmy's case, provided assistance in getting his sentence commuted and helped him enter and graduate from medical school. Dr. James (Jimmy) Bresnahan practiced medicine for the U. S. Public Health Service among California's migrant workers, but in 1999 he returned to Colorado and applied for privileges at Denver-area hospitals. He was granted temporary privileges at two hospitals but these were later withdrawn.

---

*For more information on Dr. James Bresnahan see pages 5A and 33A of the August 6, 1999, *Denver Rocky Mountain News* article entitled, "Doc tries for second chance: Man who killed parents as teen seeks privileges at Denver hospitals."

SHOWDOWN at the BULL DOMINGO MINE

The Stockholm Syndrome

She hugged the offender and forgave the offense.
-Dryden

I knew there was trouble when the phone rang at 1:00 a.m., as the control room was not to call me before 6:30 a.m. unless the commanding night officer deemed it urgent.

"Warden, we have an escape from Medium Security Cell House #2. It's O'Neal. He was missed at midnight count. You may remember him; he's a stickup doing twenty-five years. He could probably be very dangerous when on the loose."

Hanging up the phone, I hurriedly dressed and drove out to the Medium Security facility (now Fremont Correctional Facility). The hunt for the escapee had already been organized with several units searching the immediate area. I took a look at O'Neal's record to see who might have visited him lately and talked to some of the staff to see if they had detected anything unusual about his behavior. One officer thought O'Neal might have acted a bit differently while outside on the work gang, but he did his work the same as usual, so the officer had given the inmate no special attention.

After breakfast I got into my car with Lt. Dick Uhland, who was the prison firearms training officer and in charge of the armory and all firearms. We began contacting the search units by radio to see if there were any leads. One unit reported that shoe tracks with notched heels* had been found going toward Oak Creek grade southwest of Cañon City. Then at 8:15 a.m. an excited voice from the dispatcher crackled from the radio.

"Warden, there's been a kidnaping at a ranch on the north side of Oak Creek, south of the road."

Lt. Uhland kicked on the car's red lights and siren, and we sped to the ranch where the owner awaited us. A tall, thin man with a bit of gray in his hair, he was calm but tense as he told me and the other searchers his story.

At about 6:00 a.m. his fifteen-year-old daughter had gone to the well to pump a bucket of water and was accosted by a man carrying a knife. The girl brought the man (described to us as O'Neal) to the house where the rancher and his wife were cooking breakfast. The family was held hostage until about 8:30 a.m. while the escapee ate breakfast and prowled about the home, holding the young girl at knife point. Eventually he found the family weapon (an over and under, .410 above and a .22 below) and ammunition.

Vowing not to be taken alive, he said he would take the girl with him as a hostage. Her mother, a woman in her early forties, begged O'Neal to take her as hostage and leave the girl at home. After a period of debating the offer, the convict agreed, and the two left in the family car at about 9:00 a.m. with the mother driving south on the Oak Creek grade road.

Immediately after hearing this, I put out a radio description of the car and its occupants and advised everyone in radio hearing not to approach the vehicle if they spotted it. I could visualize tragic results if this desperate man and his hostage were cornered without his being able to negotiate with someone in

---

* All heels were notched on convicts' shoes to facilitate tracking of any escapee.

authority concerning his future. In simple terms, that meant me!

It was not long before we got a radio call from Dan Riggs, the Wildlife Officer in Custer County. He had spotted the car and had followed it to the road out of Silver Cliff that led to the Bull Domingo Mine. Dan directed us to his position, indicating that there was "no way out" for O'Neal and his hostage except the road they had followed to the mine. It was a dead end road.

When Lt. Uhland and I arrived at the spot, I borrowed Dan's field glasses and located the car about two miles away and uphill at the mouth of the mine. The auto had been turned around and faced back toward where we were standing, but no one was visible outside the car. The last mile to the mine was a steep grade, and the armed escapee had sight control of the entire two miles of road. It was obvious that any feasible approach would have to be made head on. The only other approach would require someone coming on foot from behind the mine and through three miles of timber.

There are times when one wonders if the job as Warden pays enough for this kind of risk, but it was too late for me to think of that. The proverbial die had been cast. We had a brave woman who had saved her daughter by sacrificing herself, facing the threat of being raped and tortured by an escapee of the prison of which I was in charge. *She had to be rescued.* Although it might have been better to be patient and try to wait out the situation, amid a bit of cold sweat, I made a decision.

"Lieutenant, wait here; we will probably have a lot of cars shortly. I'm going up the road to contact O'Neal and see if she's okay and if I can get her loose from him. Do not let him get by this roadblock with her in the car. I'll keep in touch by radio."

I got in my car and drove slowly – the longest two miles of my life. Stopping about one hundred feet from their car, I got out. It was hard to hear anything except the wind rustling through the trees on both sides of the old mine road. The woman got out on the driver's side, and O'Neal got out on the passenger side, with the rifle across his arm.

Trying to make my voice heard over the wind, with a dry mouth I yelled as authoritatively as I could, "O'Neal, let her go and come down here with your hands on top of your head!"

The woman cupped her hands to her ears as the wind prevented her from hearing me, and I motioned for her to come down the short piece of road to where I was standing. I was hopeful that O'Neal would rethink the situation and let her go.

"You are surrounded," I yelled again. "You have no way out!" (I gambled that he did not know that I was his total "surrounder.")

He hollered back, "Warden, I'm not going back to get gassed or a life sentence, so go ahead and shoot." (He could see that I was not armed,* but, apparently, he thought that there was a posse in the timber surrounding him.)

I had steadily been moving forward as we shouted and was now close enough to the lady to grab her and pull her away and down the hill. I tried to get her in my car, but she resisted!

She shocked me by saying, "Warden, if you will let me go back to David (O'Neal), I can talk him into surrendering. Please don't hurt him."

My white shirt was now wet with sweat. There I stood, unarmed, facing an armed escapee, and she was arguing with me. Gruffly, I said, "Lady, you get your damn butt in that car. *Now!*"

Ignoring my command and clinging tightly to the door handle, she refused to enter the automobile. "I'll never forgive anyone who hurts David," she whined as tears came into her eyes.

O'Neal, who was still standing with the gun in his hands,

---

* I went up the hill unarmed as I thought there would be a better chance to talk. Shootouts tend to be generated when everyone is armed.

looked around for the posse and said, "Go ahead, boss man. Have them shoot. I ain't going back!"

Behind me I now heard cars, and Lt. Bill Wilson, Capt. Jack Capelli and Lt. Uhland appeared, together with other members of search units. At that moment the escapee put the muzzle of the gun to his right side and shot himself. Lt. Wilson rushed to him and grabbed the gun as O'Neal fell to the ground. The showdown was over.

I sent the officers to the prison hospital with the wounded inmate where he underwent surgery and survived. On the way back to the ranch, the lady continued to talk about "David" as though he were her son. She came to the prison for several months afterward to see O'Neal until I finally barred her from the premises as he was attempting to use her to bring him money.

I believe this woman was a victim of the "Stockholm Syndrome" where kidnapped women are so terrified of their captors (she was a hostage for more than four hours) and are so grateful that they were not hurt or killed that they fall in a pseudo love situation with their captors. That's a simple explanation of the syndrome, but it's the best I can do and seems to explain this particular event and its conclusion.

Attorney Rollie Rogers (left) with inmate Michael Bell, who was killed in an escape attempt during the Apple Blossom Parade in Cañon City.

BLOSSOM DAY

Mid youth and song, feasting and carnival
Through laughter, through the roses, as of old
Comes death on shadowy and relentless feet.
                                    -Rupert Brooke

May 1, 1970 was sunny and warm, just a perfect day for the annual Cañon City Blossom Festival. Throughout the area the sweet fragrance of apple and cherry trees filled the air and emphasized that spring had finally arrived. Side streets in the town had been blocked off, and crowds were gathering along Main Street in anticipation of a big parade.

Resplendent in her satin finery, the Blossom Queen and her escorts were being checked as they mounted their float. Dozens of other floats of all descriptions were jockeying for position in the area near the prison. In the park on the south side and around the entire east side of the penitentiary, high school bands from all over the state of Colorado were clustered, awaiting orders to march. Garbed in colorful uniforms with plumes on their hats fluttering in the breeze, some of the young people were tuning their instruments while others laughed and talked as they awaited their turn in the parade competition.

Inside the prison walls two inmates awaited execution. Michael John Bell, age thirty-four, had been on death row since 1963 for the 1962 murder of Denver Patrolman Carl B. Knobbe. He appeared to be a mild, slightly retarded man with some artistic talent and had drawn the logo that was adopted by the Public Defenders' office. Twenty-three-year-old Ernest LeRoy Alsip, who was sentenced to death for the 1969 kidnap and murder of sixty-three-year-old Ollie Mae Jackson, had only been in the prison eleven months. A recent prisoner, he was resistant to authority and preached "skinhead" philosophy, making him more dangerous than Bell.

Apparently Bell and Alsip had decided that the Blossom Festival was the right time for an escape[*] as most of the townspeople would be caught up in the noise and excitement of the parade, and the congestion would hinder any kind of quick pursuit by law officers. They also assumed, wrongly as it turned out, that the tower guards would be distracted by the assembled high school bands.

I viewed the Blossom Day scene and listened to the sounds as I entered my office, sat down at my desk and started sorting through a pile of yesterday's mail. Suddenly, a rifle shot sounded. I called the Control Room. "Who shot?"

"Tower #8, Warden," the man responded. "And Davis on #8 says there are two men on the inside wall and they are heading for the east wall."

Immediately, I called Tower #1 (the arsenal tower) to get a pistol which was lowered to me through one of the inside elevators reserved for weapons. As this was happening, I heard three more shots being fired, and I headed for the east wall. I kicked the siren on the car, but it was tough to get through the band formations. The band kids, who were less than 100 feet from the east wall, were all laughing and pointing in that direction. However, I couldn't see anything until I noticed Associate Warden Jack Capelli standing outside his home in front of the garage with a pistol in his hand.

---

[*] For newspaper account of the escape route, see "Two Planned Escape Try," *The Denver Post*, May 3, 1971.

"Where the hell are they?" I yelled at Capelli.

"In back of the garage."

"Are they armed?" I pulled my pistol and prepared to confront the escapees.

"They're dead!" Capelli replied.

Needless to say, if these two desperate men had gotten into the crowd of band kids, the results would have been unpredictable – except I would have been searching for new employment. I could have kissed the posteriors of Capelli, Parker on Tower #6 and Wright in corner Tower #5 when Capelli said, "They're dead."

I took a look at the bodies and saw that they were condemned men Bell and Alsip.

"Call the coroner and get some blankets and sheets to shield this sight from those kids," I ordered. "Have Davis, Parker and Wright relieved and send them home.[*] Call Deputy Wyse and

* The usual procedure was to relieve officers involved in any violence.

tell him to handle the press until I know all the details. I will stay here until the coroner arrives; then I'll be in cell house #3 until we can get a handle on what happened."

I was thoroughly shocked at how these men could have escaped on to the top of the walls. The subsequent investigation brought out some amazing facts, particularly about "escape-proof" inside exercise yards. Just prior to the parade starting, the two men had been moved to an inside yard used exclusively by "death row" inmates for their daily physical exercise. During this exercise period they had only limited supervision as it was assumed the high fence and concrete floor made the yard escape proof – a dangerous assumption when used in a prison setting. However, this was soon to be proved otherwise.

Exercise yard for condemned inmates.

The key to the escape was a water faucet about four feet high against the wall where it joined cell house #3. One man with his foot on the faucet boosted the other man to the top of the wall on the yard's east edge. This man then dropped his leg down for the second man to clamber up. Quickly they scaled a chain-link fence topped by strands of barbed wire and reached the roof of a two-story wing of the death row cellblock. From there they climbed a metal ladder to the top of the three-story gas chamber, crossed that roof to a metal bridge that led to an inner wall and ran along an inner wall to the east outer wall. Suddenly, they dropped to the garage roof at the residence of Associate Warden for Custody, Jack Capelli.

The two were sighted first by Officer Don Davis in Tower #8[*] as they moved on top of Cell House #3 along a connecting bridge to an inside wall. Immediately, Officer Davis fired a warning shot into the air to alert other tower officers. Then Officer Parker in Tower #6 fired his rifle with 00 buckshot, hitting Bell in the back. The buckshot careened around his ribs and hit his heart, resulting in his death after he jumped from the garage roof and staggered a few steps. Officer Wright in Tower #5 fired buckshot which tore through the side of Alsip as he jumped to the garage where he then fell off the roof. The two dead men lay less than 100 feet from a group of band members.

Those in the bands who were interviewed afterwards thought the whole episode was just part of a show put on to entertain them while they waited for the parade to start. Some students, who had seen the men atop the wall, thought the two had a "neat place to watch a parade." Ron Neel, vocal director of the Fort Morgan High School Band indicated that many of the kids thought that the shooting incident was simply "some kind of a joke." One stated that it was "a neat show."

However, it could have turned into a "nasty show" as Bell had a homemade knife with a three-inch blade and Alsip was

---

[*] Tower #8 was an inside tower that contolled internal movement. Davis could see the east wall of the prison from his positions.

carrying an icepick-type weapon made of heavy, stiff wire. Although no one knows if others were involved in the escape attempt or exactly how long the attempt had been planned, apparently the two men hoped to merge with the band members. They assumed guards would not shoot into the assembled students, allowing them to escape by possibly seizing hostages and commandeering autos from the parade.

East outer wall and Tower # 5 after the shooting. Visiting bands can be seen at top of photo.

Both men were awaiting results of appeals to higher courts – Bell to the U.S. Supreme Court and Alsip to the Colorado Supreme Court. Perhaps the results of these appeals (and the 1976 ruling of the U.S. Supreme Court against the death penalty) might have spared their lives if they had only bided their time.

Shortly after the escape attempt, we did the usual prison response. We lowered the faucet, hung some more concertina wire and presumed that this would allow no more escape attempts.

Rollie Rogers, head of the State Public Defenders Office, asked that his client, Bell, not be buried in Woodpecker Hill. Rogers paid for Bell's burial elsewhere.

LAST DAYS
OF A TROUBLED LIFE

It was a misery to be born,
a pain through life and trouble in death.
— W.K.P.

At various times during my tenure in the correctional system, I encountered James Sherbondy, whose name became well-known because of the film *Cañon City*. Sherbondy came into the prison as a seventeen-year-old country-reared boy after having killed a deputy sheriff in Eagle county. After a few years behind bars, his focus was on freedom – escape. His best known bid for freedom was in December, 1947.

Sherbondy, along with convicts George Trujillo, Werner Schwartzmiller, John Klinger, Richard Heilman, A. B. Tolley, Orville Turley, John Smalley, R. L. Freeman, Ernest LaVergne, Harold Hathaway, and Billy Frank New, broke out of cell block #6 on December 30, 1947.[*] A woman and a prison guard were seriously wounded during the break. However, temperatures below zero and freshly-fallen snow soon forced the men to seek warm shelter. In the ensuing hunt for the escapees, Klinger and Turley were killed.

---

[*] For several days, newspapers in Cañon City, Pueblo, Colorado Springs and Denver covered the escape and capture of the prisoners in detail. For those readers interested in learning more about James Sherbondy, a book by John H. Williamson entitled, "The Gray Walls of Hell" is available in the research department of the Pueblo City County Library District.

Sherbondy took refuge a few miles north of Cañon City inthe home of George Bauer, his wife and their two children, Jerry and Myrna, both of whom were ill. Mrs. Bauer fixed Sherbondy a meal of fried eggs, soup and coffee. About four o'clock in the morning, Jerry became very sick, and Mrs. Bauer begged Sherbondy to let her take the boy to a doctor. The convict finally agreed and later was quoted in several newspapers, explaining why he had let the two leave. "I was in the house several hours ... The people had a boy about eight who was sick. They were afraid he had appendicitis ... I knew they knew who I was and would tell the cops, but I couldn't let the little kid die."

Some time later, Bauer and his daughter were able to get out of their home and drive to a house about a mile away. Bauer then telephoned Warden Roy Best who immediately sent guards to the Bauer home. Sherbondy had vowed not to be captured alive, but when the officers arrived, he surrendered without resistance.

Sherbondy's various escape attempts kept any governor from considering clemency until Sherbondy was over forty years of age. After he had been behind the walls for twenty-five years, his sentence was commuted, and he was released on parole. He teamed up with a pal from his prison days, absconded from parole, participated in a stickup, was sentenced to a term in the Illinois state prison and was returned to Colorado. His case was to be heard again by the parole board, and Jim was sent to an honor camp to await the hearing. The standard practice was that if a prisoner was turned down by the parole board, he was to be returned to the main institution to be reevaluated as to his risk to escape.

The board refused to hear Sherbondy's appeal; however, no one notified the prison of the denial. Sherbondy learned of the parole hearing outcome, vowed never to go back to prison and escaped once again from the honor farm. His search for freedom ended when he was killed in Denver in a shootout with Denver

Detective Mike Doud. Sherbondy had not been given an opportunity for parole earlier because of his own behavior. He bungled his first chance, finally gave up hope and became an extremely dangerous man.

Werner Swartzmiller after capture
following his 1947 escape with James Sherbondy.

Premier of the movie, **Cañon City.** *Roy Best is on left, next to actor Scott Brady who played the role of James Sherbondy.*

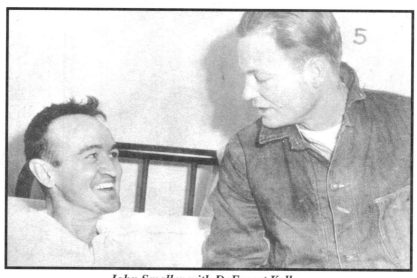

John Smalley with DeForest Kelley, who played Smalley in the movie, **Cañon City.**

The
Death Penalty

THE POWER OF
POSITIVE THINKING
Sylvester Garrison

Even a thought, even a possibility can shatter us and transform us.
- Nietzche

When I became warden of the penitentiary in 1965, there were five men facing death on "condemned row:" Joe Segura from Pueblo County, who had slain his 16-year-old son with a baseball bat when the son had tried to stop his father from beating his mother as the result of a family hassle over the canning of tomatoes; Sylvester Garrison from Denver County, convicted of assaulting and killing a jeweler in a stickup that turned violent when the jeweler resisted; Luis Monge from Denver County, convicted of killing his wife and four of his children in a bloody escapade that occurred after the mother became aware of Monge's incestuous relationship with his 15-year-old daughter; John Young from El Paso County, convicted of killing a bank employee in a bungled robbery attempt; Michael Bell from Denver County, convicted of slaying a policeman after a high-speed chase.

At that time, Garrison had been on "the row" for six years. He was a tall, light-colored black man, beginning to get a bit bald and with a sharp "V" of hair in the middle of his high forehead. During the next six years that he and I were in the prison, I found

Sylvester Garrison (center) with Denver sheriff's officers and his attorney shortly after being sentenced to death.

him to be an eternal optimist, a positive thinker who closed his mind to any negative thoughts. He had a sly sense of humor and seemed to enjoy our exchanges of bizarre jokes as his time of execution came near. We went to the "last day" twice – once a few hours before his scheduled execution.

Whenever I talked with him about his coming execution, he would just laugh and say, "You ain't ever going to get me, Boss."

I'd return the banter, saying something like, "Your luck may run out sometime," or "I'm tired of feeding you your 'last meals.'"

"Warden," he would state, "I've got to have three chickens* so the guys can eat with me. I appreciate your letting the other guys eat with me. But, Boss, you ain't never going to get me. I got a rabbit's foot, and I may live to be one hundred." All of us would have a good laugh.

---

* Garrison ate three "last meals" and got permission from me to have the other condemned men eat with him. He always ordered chicken – lots of chicken.

One Wednesday afternoon I called Garrison over to the Deputy Warden's office and told him, "Sylvester, unless I hear something from the courts by Friday at 8:00 P.M., you're going to leave this world. Both Father Justin and Reverend Riske* have indicated that they will be available on a twenty-four-hour basis if you wish. I suggest that you make your peace with your God and prepare yourself to enter eternity."

"Boss, I've done prepared myself," Garrison responded, "but it just ain't going to happen, and it will be legal you won't have to drag me into that 'bug killer.'"

As scheduled, we tested the chamber and prepared to execute Garrison on Friday evening. Then at about 4:00 P.M., Justice Byron White of the U.S. Supreme Court called me with a "stay of execution." Sylvester was eating his "last meal" and had a good laugh as the deputy sent all of the execution squad home.

I could never understand how Garrison (or anyone) could maintain his sanity on death row. For twelve years (4,380 days), he had no friends from the outside and could only talk to his lawyer or the other death row inmates. He saw nothing of the outside world, but a bit of sky when he visited my office or the deputy's office, and there were always silent men watching his every move. Yet Sylvester maintained a positive attitude and made it work. Did it save his life? He thought so!

Garrison was freed as a result of the 1972 Supreme Court decision nullifying the death penalty as then practiced. He secured a job as a maintenance man in the Denver City and County building, and, during the time that I ran the Sheriff's office in Denver, he visited me regularly. He was always the positive talker and thinker, and we had some great visits. Amid the darkness he always saw a ray of light!

---

* Garrison never expressed a religious preference.

*The preparation room where the condemned was kept
prior to the walk to the gas chamber.*

MY MAMA

Susan Emma (Maxson) Patterson

To every thing there is a season,
and a time for every purpose under Heaven . . .
a time to live and a time to die . . .
- Holy Bible

Someone once said, "All the good characteristics of men are endowed to them by their mother." I suspect that persistent moral feelings that have pursued and troubled me over my life were the result of my mother's teaching.

To gain a perspective on how this prison story evolved, the reader needs to have some insight into my mother's personality and her belief in what was right or wrong. Mother was reared (and reared her family) in the Seventh Day Baptist religion, a very old branch of the denomination of Baptists, differing from the parent body in observing

Saturday, instead of Sunday, as the seventh day of the week and as the Sabbath. In England they were called "Sabbatarians."

However, Mother's interest did not center only around religion. She was a dedicated baseball fan all of her life. She could give you the batting averages of nearly everyone in the big leagues – Babe Ruth, Gehrig, Hornsby, Mantle, Pepper Martin and the era of Schoolboy Rowe, Lefty Grove, Dizzy Dean, Koufax or Palmer. You name them, and Mother could give you their stats. She listened to radio broadcasts of games, avidly read the sports pages, rooted for her favorites and castigated old time managers for their strategy. Her eyesight began to fail in her later years, but she spent the afternoons close up to the television on baseball days. I doubt if she missed seeing or hearing a World Series, if they were broadcast.

In her younger days she loved to play sandlot baseball with her boys and their pals. The neighborhood kids would yell and clap when she showed up at the game. At just five feet tall and 135 pounds, she was a tough competitor. She had a great sense of fun and humor, and sometimes we had great times laughing together.

Still, Mother was a pure warrior against anything that she perceived as evil. In her long battles with Satan and his evils, she was a lifetime member of the Women's Christian Temperance Union (WCTU). She fought many battles against those she referred to as "the booze peddlers" and the drinkers as "sots and wife beaters." Anything that seemed to be an alcoholic beverage was on her "hit list." Root beer and near beer were not allowed on the premises. When I, in jest, would remind her that Jesus Christ had turned water into wine, she insisted that it was unfermented juice of the grape. In a fight, Mother gave no quarter nor did she expect any from the Devil's disciples.

Long before "women's lib" was dreamed about, Mother was an active proponent of women's right to vote and to a career.

She was a longtime supporter of the ACLU until they filed a suit that she saw as an attack on religion.* She crusaded against smoking, not because she thought it was a health threat but because she thought it was an evil that damaged the body – the temple that housed the soul.

In her early years my mother was an educator and, although her own pursuit of a professional career was destroyed by the advent of a family of five boys and one girl (with no government day care centers available), she continued to write numerous letters to politicians, public figures and newspaper editors about the evils of the world which "they were allowing to happen." In addition, she wrote – to my dismay at times – to prisoners and other perceived evildoers in an all-out attempt to save their wicked souls.

Mother was an implacable foe of the death penalty and adhered to Biblical teachings, mostly from the *New Testament*. She believed that human life was a pretty precious commodity because, again, it was "the temple of the soul." She felt that judgments as to who lived or died were not for mere mortals to decide but were solely within the purview of the Divine. (Although I became more cynical and worldly as I pursued my career, I am still prone to believe that message which was drilled into my mind by my mother.) Because of her beliefs, she became a "player" in the following prison execution.

In May 1967, after the defeat of a referendum on the death penalty in Colorado, I was discussing the resetting of death dates with five condemned prisoners. To my dismay, one of the men, Segura, showed me a letter from my mother, who at that time was eighty-two years old. Among other statements my mother had written to him, "The State can take away your bodies but it can't take away your souls." It was only then that I discovered that

---

* The final blow to her support of the ACLU was when the organization threatened to sue my administration.

Mother had been corresponding with *all* the condemned men. I was somewhat shocked when I thought that I, her third son, was the Officer of the State that she was indicating would "take away their bodies."

After the condemned men had left the office, I called the Mail Officer, Sgt. Vickman, to inquire as to why I was not appraised of this strange circumstance. Shaking his head, Sgt. Vickman explained, "Warden, I didn't know that Susie Patterson writing from Denver was your mother, and she was writing beautiful and hopeful letters* to these men. Besides, you told me to be lenient with the mail to the condemned men." He was correct. I had made that directive.

A few months later, on June 2, 1967, condemned prisoner Luis Monge was in the final preparation cell** awaiting his execution. During the usual strained silence of the preparation cell, as the doctors were placing the electrodes to his legs, Monge's voice shattered the silence. "Doctor, will this gas bother my asthma?" he asked. Monge knew this was a tense time for everyone, and he may have thought his question would ease the nerves of the two doctors, Chaplain Father Justin and me. After a long, shaky silence, one of the doctors finally said, "Not for long."

Monge, who had been sentenced for the murder of his wife *** was guilt ridden and had not fought against being put to death. As he got up to go into the death chamber, I saw that he carried in his hand a small picture of Christ at the crucifixion.

---

* Mail addressed to prisoners was opened, but not censored, by prison officials prior to being delivered to the inmates. The practice went back in history and was used to deter inmates' efforts at smuggling, escapes, etc.

** A cell located outside the gas chamber room where the condemned was stripped except for underwear and had electrodes attached for later attachment of the electrocardiograph.

*** The survivors of Monge's family (five children) remained loyal to him, visited and shared his last meal.

Offering it to me for inspection, he asked, "Warden, may I take this to the chamber with me?"

I looked at the picture and saw that it was framed by a unique design made from the wrappings of cigarette packages which had been intricately folded. Seeing no threat to the State's plan for taking his life and assuming the picture had some religious meaning for him, I said, "Sure, go ahead."

We then proceeded to the gas chamber, and after Monge was strapped into the chair, Father Justin, wrapped a rosary around his wrist and moved outside. Before a hood was placed on Monge's head, I stepped into the chamber to elicit any last words and to wish him well as he entered eternity. "Warden," Monge began, "one last favor?"

"Yes," I replied, "if it's within my power."

He then handed me the picture of Christ and said, "Give this to your mother and God bless her. She wanted us all to live. You are a good man and a good warden. Goodbye."

Preparations for an execution required great concentration and exact timing on the part of all those involved. Sixteen people were required to perform the act with sixteen more on reserve as backup. Release of the cyanide was controlled by a lever with the handle immobilized by a steel pin which ran through the lever handle. This method of immobilization avoided an accidental movement that might prematurely execute someone before the time set by the courts or by the governor's decision to intervene.

The deputy warden would stand clear of the gas chamber and the official witnesses and would signal when the doctors had connected the cardiogram and had it in working order. At the signal, my assistant officer would remove the pin from the lever. I would then check the clock and at 8:01 p.m. be ready to release the cyanide eggs into the acid. A telephone line was kept open to the governor in case of a last-minute commutation of the sentence.

The pressure of those last few minutes when Monge handed me that picture was worse than all of the previous preparations and the actual execution. The passing of the picture was witnessed by members of the media and other witnesses to the execution, and I was immediately deluged with questions: "What did Monge give to you? What did he say? Why did he give you something?" On June 5, 1967, *The Denver Post* carried the following story:

Last Possession Sent To Warden's Mother

Just before his execution Friday night, Luis Jose Monge gave away his last worldly possession – to the mother of his jailer. Wayne K. Patterson, warden of the Colorado State Penitentiary, said the gift was a picture of the crucifixion in a hand-made frame which Monge had woven from strips of Pall Mall cigarette wrappers. One the back of the picture Monge wrote:

"To Mrs. B. P. Patterson. Thank you for your kind thoughts and prayers. God bless you.

Luis J. Monge"

Radio, television and the newspapers had a field day with the story. *The executioner's mother was writing to and consoling condemned prisoners!* The incident became a media topic for several years and caused me some little consternation.

However, my mother was not to be deterred. She continued to correspond with the other condemned men in spite of strong pressure from our family to cease doing so. She seemed delighted when the other condemned men were not executed.* For all of her public letters and bouts with the Devil and his aides, Susan Patterson never forgot to be a mother to all of those she felt needed her.

---

* In 1972 the Supreme Court declared the death penalty law unconstitutional.

*Warden Patterson running a test of the gas chamber
for a proposed execution. Usually a pig was used
during the test to gauge response to lethal gas.*

QUESTIONS AND ANSWERS
on the
THE DEATH PENALTY

The questions listed below were gleaned from memory and have been asked of me or heard by me over a long period of years. My answers are my own, and the reader must remember the time frame to which many of these answers apply. However, I believe my answers would be very similar today.

-WKP (2003)

• *Wouldn't the death penalty be more effective as a deterrent to crimes if used more?*

A. This argument seems to me to ignore thousands of years of bloody history. Somewhere I once read that during the reign of Henry VIII (1509-1547) some 72,000 were executed in England. These executions were carried out in hideous ways, enormous volume and as publicly as possible, yet this failed to change the criminal activity or political opposition.

• *Shouldn't the death penalty be retained as a retributive weapon against atrocious criminals? Serial murderers?*

A. Yes, if you have a modified version of the penalty. If you oppose the death penalty, opposition must be unqualified.

• *If the death penalty were abolished, what would be an appropriate penalty for murder? Treason? Possibly life without parole?*

A. Life without parole – a drastic and lasting punishment. However, the general public is not sold on this alternative. (See my description of life without parole at the end of this treatise.)

• *Would not long and complicated legal battles be avoided if the maximum penalty was life? If there were no death penalty, wouldn't this save a great deal of money?*

A. Not necessarily; life without parole would be aggressively litigated.

• *Historically and statistically, "one time" murderers have been, by far, the safest risk on parole. Doesn't this serve redemptive justice and the public safety better while, as a society, raising our moral and humane values?*

A. Yes, but it is hard to make the general public believe this. The idea fortifies their belief that murderers are released indiscriminately soon after they are given a LIFE sentence. The public seems to believe that life without parole does not mean what it says.

• *Is it really acceptable to say in our supposedly advanced, civilized society that the deaths are extracted to protect the rest of the society, prevent repetition of the crime and serve as a warning to others? Or, do we say that we took the life in the name of justice and revenge?*

A. Political leaders say this, and because they say this, the people believe what is asked in the first sentence. Most district attorneys like "the name of justice." The question we might ask is: How advanced are civilized are we?

• *Why support some murderer for the rest of his life when we could execute him and save all that money?*

A. I don't believe that execution is cheaper than life in prison. There are the actual costs of an execution to be considered – the cost of operating a super maximum security unit, the number of years spent by some prisoners in condemned status, a pro-rata share of the cost of top level prison officials' time spent in administering the unit, etc. Probably half of the condemned could be highly useful prisoners working in industrial, maintenance or clerical roles at about half the salary of a regular employee. They would be able to pay for their own keep and also the keep of the other half of those condemned. Also, other costs can be cited – sanity proceedings, automatic appeals and other appeals, the time of the governor and his staff. Economy is on the side of abolition.

• *From a public safety standpoint, which might be more effective – abolition of the penalty or its disuse?*

A. Hard to answer. Over the past thirty years, Colorado has voted to keep it as the law, but seems reticent about using it.

• *Is the death penalty only an arbitrary discrimination against an occasional victim, without effect on crime?*

A. Yes, in my opinion. However, the pro-penalty folks argue that it has an effect on crime by preventing the culprit from repeating the crime.

• *What about having the death penalty only for killing police officers or correctional officers?*

A. They are the ones in the most hazardous positions and should have all the protections society can give them. But abolition requires that lives not be evaluated one against the other.

- *Does our daily diet of killing and other forms of violence on TV or other media have any effect on our views of the death penalty?*

    A. Yes. It seems to promote the idea that killing someone is no big deal. Reality is only on the fringe of perception. Also some media programs seem to promote the notion that there are possibly some folks that need killing.

- *If murder is evil, do we not compound the evil by taking a life in return?*

    A. In some people's eyes. But in whose eyes? Evil becomes good in the eyes of the public when the offender is executed.

- *Do our old, built-in, vengeful prejudices keep us from recognizing the truth about the deterrent value of the death penalty?*

    A. I believe so. Politicians and their public following are affected, or infected, with that which I call "invincible ignorance" as to crime control. (I used to say this publicly and draw some ire but could find no better grasp of the subject by anyone – at least that I could detect.)

- *If death is the most terrifying thing that a human being can face, isn't it common sense and logic that the fear of death is the greatest deterrent to the commission of a murder?*

    I had also heard this questioned in a legislative hearing by a noted attorney of that day. Under that interpretation of common sense and logic, he would have had to avoid the freeways, where death is a driving companion. The possibility of his death on the highway would have been a deterrent.

    A. I have interviewed a lot of murderers during my time in public service and have never heard one say that he contemplated the death penalty before he committed the crime. None ever contemplated getting caught! The penalty enters the picture <u>after</u> the villain is caught.

• Why haven't criminologists, statisticians and psychiatrists or other professionals been able to convince legislators and the public of the futility of the death penalty, if, indeed, it is futile?

A. They are scientists, intellectuals and students – not salesmen – and besides, their audience is mostly "invincibly ignorant." (See above.)

• Is the death penalty equally applied? Is it a just penalty, as in the word "justice"?

A. No, not in my opinion, but maybe to some it is considered justice. I have known many during my time who committed crimes more fiendish than those people who were executed. Some of those who committed the more horrendous crimes are now free.

• Is the death penalty reparative? Does it repay the victim or the victim's family? What is meant by the new media words "providing closure" for the victim's family?

A. No, I don't feel it is reparative. As to an answer for the last question, I don't know the answer. Perhaps it lets some of the families "get even" for the loss of a loved one. An eye for an eye.

• Is murder for which the death penalty is applicable, ordinarily a repetitive crime which the perpetrator must be permanently enjoined from repeating?

A. In my judgment, no. During my stewardship in several correctional positions I saw 100 men and 2 women under life sentences. A life sentence at that time meant life, except for clemency by the governor. Ten of these individuals became insane or died in prison. Ninety men and the 2 women were released on parole after periods of confinement of 12 to 35 years. Two men

151

were returned for alcohol-related parole violations. None were returned for repeat homicides.

• *Is it possible that an innocent person could be executed?*

A. Yes, of that particular crime. However, with the advent of new scientific tools available to criminal justice personnel, it is not probable.

• *Is the threat of the death penalty so severe to the defendant's mind that he will plead guilty to any offense of a lesser penalty, guilty or not, to escape legal execution? Doesn't this compromise fair justice?*

A. It does happen that someone would plead guilty to a lesser offense in order to escape execution, but most often this occurs when the individual is guilty. In answer to the second question, justice is compromised if the individual is not guilty.

• *Does the long lag between the death sentence and its execution negate the deterrent effects of the penalty?*

A. Yes, if one assumes there are any deterrent effects. There is an old saying: For punishment to be effective, it must be swift, certain and not disproportionate to the offense.

• *If the death penalty weren't in the law, would we have vigilantes practicing executions in its place?*

A. It could happen and has happened. We are descendants of some pioneer folks who responded to violence with violence.

• *What is wrong with having the death penalty in the law to assist prosecuting attorneys to get plea bargains and avoid long, expensive trials?*

A. Many people have opinions on this; however, it only affects a minute number of crimes and a small number of criminal prosecutions. Appeals usually follow, and no criminals seem to be happy with the punishment they have meted out to them.

• *Are minorities more apt to be subjected to the death penalty than whites? Is there some social reason?*

A. Yes to the first question, and I don't know to the second. Perhaps the position of minorities in the system causes pressure not experienced by whites, resulting in more violence-related crimes and proportionally more homicides.

• *Is it true that persons of wealth never get the death penalty? They commit capital crimes, don't they?*

A. I don't personally recall anyone of wealth getting the penalty. Yes, they also commit crimes. I do recall several serious murders committed by wealthy men who got short second degree murder sentences.

• *Are mentally retarded individuals (or developmentally disabled as they are referred to now) and mentally ill murderers given full consideration of their mental condition when the death penalty is being assessed?*

A. In some cases they are; however, I have known of cases of mentally ill or retarded who were executed.

• *If we believe that the death penalty deters crime, why don't we enhance it by returning to public executions?*

A. If the penalty stays on the books, it probably should be more public. The public should be fully advised as to the reality of the death penalty.

• *Is any method of execution of the death penalty more humane than another?*

A. No! You are dead when it's over, and any method can be "botched" and cause pain. The law requires punishment, and the dictionary says this means "to suffer for the offense."

• *What is the apparent overriding reason for the retention of the death penalty?*

A. Retribution and revenge.

Our entire criminal justice system is predicated on the theory that punishment is the answer to the complicated problem of crime. Individuals who commit society's most horrendous crimes are either locked up forever or executed. Those citizens who debate the issue of death versus life without parole need to take a look at just what both entail.

The Death Penalty

The victim is escorted into a small room with official witnesses seated behind a curtained window. The person to be executed is then strapped to a frame and laid upon a gurney. Medical needles connected through the opposite wall to vials of lethal fluid are inserted into the arms. The curtains are opened, allowing other witnesses to have a full view of the execution. When the signal is given, the vials of fluid are injected, causing death. The victim simply goes to sleep.

Life Without Parole

For the balance of his or her life, the inmates:

• will be deprived of freedom, the right we most cherish in our democracy.

• will be required to live in a home the size of and with the accoutrements of a bathroom – maybe with a partner with unpleasant habits, someone who would never have been chosen as a "roommate" if there had been any choice.

• will have no choice as to when or what they eat.

• will have no choice as to the type of work they will be required to do.

• will have neighbors who are destructive and dangerous.

• will be deprived of the company of the opposite sex. (A young member of the same sex may begin to look quite attractive. Inmates will be sexually harrassed or become a sexual harrasser – or both.)

• will be severely restricted in correspondence and visiting privileges with relatives and friends.

• will have the entire world – usually a few acres of barren landscape – surrounded by walls, high fences and razor wire which will hide any view of "free world" activity.

• will learn (like Pavlov's dogs) to respond to bells, whistles and loud speakers during waking hours.

• will hear the tread of the night keeper and see his flashlight during sleeping hours.

• will have no keys for doors as these are controlled by the "keepers."

• will not have a choice of which doctor or hospital to utilize should illness befall.

• will constantly be thinking of and searching for ways of escape, although these thoughts may diminish with age.

• will find that family relationships and friendships fade away over the years.

• will possibly end up suffering from some form of mental illness.

• will eventually suffer ill health and find that a prison hospital becomes a final home.

• will leave this life, probably unloved and unmourned, to be given a pauper's funeral and rest in a pauper's grave.

If all of the above sounds hopeless, it is! Personally, I'd take the sleep of the lethal injection to life without parole – if I had to make a choice.

The ANATOMY of an EXECUTION
by ASPHYXIATION
from LETHAL GAS

Lethal Gas Chamber Preparation

Manufacturer's recommendation was that the following be performed if the chamber had not been used for several months

1.   Tighten all nuts around windows and below floor.

2.   Check all cotter keys and lever pins.

3.   Start fan and check for vacuum.

4.   Using a candle, check thoroughly for leaks from outside.

5.   Run water through the mixing chamber and fill same to floor level.

6.   Check below floor for leaks.

7.   Check equipment for ammonia use.

8.   Recheck and double check the day of use!!

Appoint the following operators

1.   Chamber operator and backup

2.   Chemical operator and backup

3.   One acid man and one backup

4. One cyanide egg man and one backup

5. Two hood and strap men and two backups

6. Two doctors, one electrocardiogram, one general observation

7. Two telephone operators, one main board and one in execution room

8. Two escorts for official witnesses

9. Two escorts for media

10. One chaplain, one backup

11. One escort for prisoner (warden) and one backup

12. One for press telephone outlets, one backup

13. One at standby generator and one backup

14. One ranking officer for doors and overall observation

15. Deputy in charge of team

Testing with a walk through without stand-in (two)

Testing with a stand-in (one)

Timing: By law the warden sets the time within the week ordered by the court.

Agreed time - 8:00 p.m. Friday of week ordered by court.

1. Governor and director notified of time fixed.

2. Watches coordinated warden, deputy to team.

3. 6:45 – Recheck all systems and ready the chamber.

4. 7:00 – Deputy notifies warden that all systems are ready.

5. Witnesses and media escorted to chamber – official witnesses to the front of the chamber, media and others to the viewing room behind the chamber.

6. 7:20 – Warden travels to condemned row, reads death warrant and escorts prisoner to preparation cell.

7. 7:35 – Prisoner strips, dons shorts and has electrodes attached by doctor to chest, arms and legs.

8. 7:45 – Prisoner enters chamber, electrocardiogram attached.

9. 7:50 – Prisoner hoodwinked and strapped into chair.

10. 7:55 – Last rites and last words with Warden.

11. 8:00 – Door closed, last minute check with doctors.

12. Warden checks time and with telephone in room.

13. Pin that frees the level is removed. Lever is pulled and eggs are immersed in the acid.

14. All actions of prisoner are recorded until the attending doctor pronounces him dead.

15. Gas in the chamber is then neutralized and expelled.

16. Body is then removed to the morgue where an autopsy is performed.

The view from the back of the gas chamber
with a guard acting as a stand in
during the testing phase before an execution.
This view would be seen
by those witnessing an execution.

Trouble
in the Cell Houses

THE SUNDAY RACIAL RHUBARB
February 21, 1972

A little rebellion now and then is a good thing.
Like storms in the spring that end in a rainbow,
they awaken all prison workers to the reality of their dangerous work.
                                                              -WKP

It was Sunday – a day of rest. Mary and I were planning to go out for lunch at Gus Salardino's when the phone rang. That cancelled the rest, the luncheon and any further plans for that day in February. The voice on the other end of the phone was Lt. Green calling from "Midway" inside the prison.

"Warden, we have a bad situation here. We just had a 'sticking' in cell house #7. A Chicano hit a black man, and now the Chicano is keeping us out of the cell house. Also, there are a big crowd of whites and Chicanos running around the cell house." Green paused for a moment and then continued, "Cell house seven officer says he is staying in the cage, and he thinks they have been drinking Pruno.* Now that militant black from California, Farly, has gathered a group of blacks up in the big yard, and he is stirring up a storm. I've got the big gate** closed and locked, but the gangs are howling and demonstrating on both sides

---

* A nickname given to the illicit drink made by convicts from purloined prunes, sugar and yeast.

** A large fencing gate that connected the cell house area from the big yard.

of the gate. We need help! We can't get the ambulance into the west gate, because there is another gang there yelling threats, and the injured black is still in cell house #7."

"Blow the whistle," I directed, "and I'll be there in a few minutes. I'll come through the west gate."

The situation was just as Lt. Green had described to me. Immediately I did a number of things: first, I had the west gate Salle Port opened and directed the ambulance to cell house #7, with me riding in it. The crowd at the west gate scattered to keep from being run down by the ambulance. Once there, I got several officers, and we carried the injured prisoner out and sent him to the hospital. This took some time as the injured man had fallen on the third tier, and prisoners were yelling and throwing things. Then I had one of my favorite officers, Ray Roetker, volunteer to follow me around "watching my back." (A little bit of humor was involved here as this officer had been having a few drinks at a local bar, but when he heard the whistle, he had immediately responded and volunteered to come with me.) So far the inmates were only involved in yelling, throwing soda cans and making threats, but it was very reassuring to have Ray behind me during this tense confrontation.

In response to the whistle blowing, a large group of off-duty officers had arrived at the prison, and the afternoon captain, Nelson Goertz, took over with his radio. The convicts at the west side of the gate now began to break windows in the canteen. I told Captain Goertz to instruct the north tower man to fire into the ground in front of the canteen. When he did this, the attack stopped, and nearly half of the mob dispersed, leaving about one hundred at the gate. The blacks went to the Big Yard where the leader, Farley, continued to incite the crowd of blacks to raise clenched fists and to demonstrate.

At about this same time, Lt. Green told me that Lt. Bill Wilson was in the auditorium with nearly a thousand convicts, attending the Sunday movie which was due to end in a few minutes. To release a thousand cons from the movie into the already tense situation could have led to disaster. "Get Lt. Wilson on the radio," I told Capt. Goertz, "and tell him to hold all of them in the auditorium until we can get control out here."

Suddenly, out of the group of whites and Hispanics on the west side of the big gate, a wild-eyed convict named Jimmy Line came charging up to me carrying a long "shank," which looked to me like a pitchfork tine with a taped handle. "Warden, we are going to take you hostage,"* he yelled.

While I was contemplating the shank and sweating a bit, behind me Roetker said in a loud voice, " Line, did you see that hearse that was in front of seven?" Line did not reply, but his eyes bulged and he appeared ready to fight. "Well, if "The Man"** even winks at the tower officer, he'll blow your ass right into that hearse!" Line made a quick decision. He faded back into the crowd and kept his mouth shut. (The shank was later found in a trash can in cell house #7, and Line was sent to isolation.)

Just then, Associate Warden Capelli and several other officers came in the front entrance carrying a Thompson sub-machine gun which he accidentally fired with an attention-getting loud "bang." I took the loud speaker and, as I recall, I said, "Now, everyone get into your cells before someone gets killed or badly hurt. In five minutes I am ordering all towers to start firing and to kill those who are not in their cell or in the cell houses." The threat had its effect; they all headed for the cell houses.

Lt. Green came up to me about ten minutes later and stated, "Warden, the officers in cell house one say the men are not going into their cells. They are *in* the cell house but not going into the cells."

---

* There was little chance of the rioters taking me hostage as I was standing under the north tower, and a raised hand by me would have caused Line to be shot, but it was a scary thought.

** The warden was often referred to by both officers and convicts as "The Man" – usually not in his presence.

"Send an officer to the top of the cell house cupola on the roof," I responded, "and tell him to fire into the floor of the cell house." The officer did as directed, and there was no more problem getting the occupants into their cells!*

Shortly thereafter, Lt.Wilson released the movie crowd, and they went peacefully to their cells. The near riot was settled, and the Sunday day of "rest" was over, except for a couple of hours spent on the telephone answering media calls and fifteen minutes in an interview with Al Nakkula of *The Rocky Mountain News*.

---

* I found out later that the shot fired to the floor had sent a chip of cement flying through the air which had hit an inmate who was not in his cell. He was not seriously hurt, but apparently, the incident got the attention of the other inmates!

SEVEN DAYS IN NOVEMBER
The Insurrection of 1971

Wisdom makes slow progress in dealing with disturbances in prisons,
but prevails when humane controls are maintained
– until the violence wanes.
- WKP, 1971

On November 1, 1971, a sudden mutiny occurred in the prison. The protestors of the 1960s had seemed to have called a truce between themselves and their keepers and had been peaceful. A fist fight was a big event and an act of violence was a unique happening, until November 1, 1971 when the uprising among the prisoners destroyed nearly two years of comparative peace in the facility.

Therefore, the mutiny of the prisoners was a shocking and mind-bending experience for all staff. It forced the administration and the staff into seven days of a tense, hostile relationship with over 1,350 prisoners. That seven days tested the courage and professional loyalties of the staff and their sense of humane treatment of their charges.

Uprisings or riots often occur in a chain pattern, beginning at one institution and then spreading to other institutions over a period of months. In early September of 1971, the prisoners in Attica, New York revolted and took control of the prison. They maintained internal control of the institution, made inflammatory speeches, took hostages, threatened more violence and forced officials to negotiate with a large group of outside sympathizers. Finally, on the fourth day of the riot, the correctional officers and the State Police launched an assault against the rioters, resulting in the deaths of forty-three individuals – thirty-four rioters and nine officer hostages. The public was shocked and angered.

Shortly thereafter, disturbances with varying degrees of violence erupted in Kansas, Nebraska and New Mexico. At that time I was the President of the Wardens' Association of America and called each of the wardens of the states involved to offer the assistance of the association. They kept me posted on the actions taken during their disturbances. I, in turn, kept our top staff aware of the methods used to control their uprisings. In addition, I attended meetings at the national level where participants were trying to find some answers to the problem of how facilities could avoid or control an uprising. Correctional officers sensed that we were seeing a change in internal control and a new resistance to authority by the convicts that could result in more serious disturbances.

The media had given wide coverage to the disturbances in the various states, and the Colorado prisoners began to identify with those prisoners' demands as they were publicized. We at Cañon City were able to observe the growing signs of unrest but failed to meet or deal with it. The prisoners, with full access to radio, newspapers and magazines, began to have imagined grievances fostered by the demands in other states that had been granted.

Through the 1960s, the prison had been absorbing a large number of prisoners spawned by the organized protests and demonstrations of that period. As the following profile shows, these were a new breed of prisoners, mirroring the outside society at that time. They:

- were young, eighteen to twenty-five.
- were generally well-educated and politically smart.

- were overly impressed with *their* "rights" but not very interested in the rights of others.

- came to the prison after what they considered successful protests against the Vietnam War, the authority of colleges and universities and the government.

- perceived prisons and jails as the ultimate in corrupt government's ability to confine and eliminate dissidents.

- saw themselves as political prisoners and gave no consideration to law violations.

- were drug culture oriented. Selling, sharing and smoking pot was no crime.

- had strong outside drug contacts.

- were impulsive actors which made them dangerous and difficult to manage in the closed society of the prison. (Old time convicts were plotters and planners but seldom acted on impulse.)

The prisoners began to be demanding and agitating. The officers began to resist policies that they saw as giving in to prisoner demands. Officer morale started to dwindle, and the officers formed some union activity groups. Soon, the prison became like a caldron, simmering until it finally reached a boiling point. Prison unrest had finally come to Colorado.

We, the administration and staff, were faced with reality. Had we learned anything from the trouble in the other prisons? Was there some way we could defuse the situation? I called a meeting to discuss the problem, but the prisoners called for a strike the same day, November 1. Could Attica happen at the Colorado State Penitentiary? I announced to the media, "Yes! It certainly could."

The prisoners gathered in the Big Yard to plot their strategy. I walked up to Midway* and could hear Britt, the head of the kitchen crew, in the Big Yard yelling at the top of his lungs. "All right, you dumb ass convicts. You want to protest the food.** Go ahead! The kitchen crew is on strike right now, and there will be no dinner tonight." (Britt was the head cook and a tough black. He had worked in the kitchen for several years and resented having the crew of over 100 convicts insulted by loud protestors complaining about the food.) "I've been in four prisons, and this is the best food that you'll find anywhere," he bellowed.

At this same time I detected a breach in the rioters' unit – a good sign. The staff had also noticed that the smart, old-time convicts had that afternoon quietly bought every food item available in the prison canteen.

As administrators and staff, we made no move until the prisoners had returned to their cells – with no dinner. Then, I ordered a complete lockdown and drafted some procedures to be followed the next day. One of the leaders, a convicted murderer named Kostal, had told me that they intended to emerge the next morning and stage a "sitdown" until they could get the media to hear their side of the disturbance and force the administration into negotiating a long list of grievances. The lockdown stayed in place seven days while the prisoners pursued their efforts to gain control of the institution and dictate the terms of future programs. I then issued orders to all personnel:

- The lockdown would remain effect until further orders.

- Medical personnel and classification officers were to see that every prisoner on medication was given his medication at the proper time, in his cell. No cell was to be opened except on orders of the Warden, Deputy Warden or Shift Captain.

---

* The checkpoint and control office near the center of the prison.

** Some of the inmates had been complaining about the food, and the kitchen crew resented this as they felt they were preparing good meals.

- Prisoners could shout and continue to toss trash from their cells, but there would be no retaliation. We would keep rigid control until their enthusiasm waned.

- Their list of demands would be released to the media, but no interviews would be permitted with *anyone* – media or lawyers. All requests for interviews by attorneys were to be referred to me.

- No pictures and no cameras were to be allowed inside except those of prison photographers, and these were to be retained in the photo department.

- All staff would remain on their regular shifts, but assignments would vary as necessary to keep the institution on a schedule. The boiler house and kitchen would be manned by officers – no convicts.

- Sandwiches would be offered daily to all prisoners, and a count of the number consumed daily would be kept.

- Regardless of the prisoners' behavior, "Kill their wrath with kindness and humane treatment" was the order of the day.

- The State of Colorado would be in charge when the insurrection was over, so there was to be no retaliation.

- Prisoners were allowed to listen to the radio,* but no television or newspapers were permitted.

I had called Governor Love and advised him of the situation and was told, "Warden, you handle it, and I'll be here if you need me." I set up an open line to him twice daily, and once a day I called to the Director of Institutions, Hilbert Schauer.

---

* Inmates were allowed to listen to the local radio station, but when the station broadcast only the administration's version of the news, the inmates would erupt. At those times I ordered that there be no contact with the outside world.

After that was accomplished, we set ourselves up for a siege of undetermined length. A command post with closed-circuit television was established in the outer area, and a briefing was held every morning with reports given to the incoming employees as to what had occurred during the previous shift. Media reporters waiting out the standoff were given a briefing by either myself or Deputy Warden Wyse. The list of prisoner demands was released, but no interviews with the demonstrators were permitted.

All of the officers and staff jumped in to tend to the daily cooking, cleaning and housekeeping. We found untapped talent in other vocations among the officers. Ex-military men knew kitchen duty. One officer was an expert baker. Several meat cutters emerged and were welcomed to help with the chores.

Daily, several hundred sandwiches were put together and offered to the locked down prisoners. The consumption of these sandwiches was viewed by me as a barometer of zeal of the prisoners to continue their attempt to dramatize their demands. Since the non-participants were afraid of the insurgency leaders and their network of "snitches," only three sandwiches were taken on the first day. Day two, twenty-one were taken. Day three, 320 were devoured. The fourth day 615 were taken; day five, the count was up to 670, and on the sixth day 1012 were passed through the bars.

During this time, the classification officers had made most of the personal contacts with the prisoners and had endured endless verbal abuse. The inmates shouted epithets, beat on the bars with cups, screamed, threw all sorts of material out of their cells, plugged the toilets and sewer system, set fires and created an orchestrated tumult for most of the first three days and nights.

On the second night I walked into cell house #1. Those on the lower tier became quiet as I passed their cells, but the upper tier prisoners screamed louder. The cell house was full of smoke, and three small fires were burning in front of the lower tier.

An officer yelled at me, "Duck, Warden." He was coming along one tier with a leaky fire hose that was spewing water in every direction except through the nozzle. I ducked! Smoke from the fires was so bad in the upper tiers that I was tempted to open the huge fans in the roof to exhaust the smoke. However, with fires still blazing in some spots, a serious conflagration could have been induced by operating the fans. Finally, an officer using the loud speaker in the block got the prisoners' attention and advised them to stop setting fires and we would operate the fans. They stopped, and the fans helped clear the tier.

As I ducked under the layer of smoke during my trip up and down the tier, I noticed that Everett (an ex-lawyer) was banging away on a typewriter. Smoke was drifting into his cell, so he would cough once in a while and then continue to type. I asked, "Everett, what in hell are you typing?" He turned and said, "I'm preparing a writ against you for your refusal to negotiate these reasonable demands." I had to laugh in spite of the chaos surrounding me.

Then I made my way to cell house #6 as I had been advised that all of the

Everett Small brought suit against Warden Patterson.
Photo courtesy of George Crouter

outside windows in the cell house had been broken out. It was cold, and I was tempted to make it uncomfortable for the convicts by leaving the windows as they were. However, I had ordered

<u>no retaliation</u>, so I had the broken windows covered with plastic and issued extra blankets to the convicts who requested them.

The fourth day of the insurrection, Alex Wilson, the Associate Warden at the medium security facility and the ranches, called me and said that 300 convicts had gone outside the cell houses and refused to re-enter, saying that they were on a sympathy strike.

"They haven't caused much damage yet," Wilson reported, "but they are growing more rebellious and making weapons – knives, ball bats, football helmets, clubs and various other things – and indicating they are intending to escalate the rioting."

The battle was now on another front and had to be dealt with. I called the Governor and Gil Carrel, Chief of the State Patrol, and got permission to use the Patrol riot control squad to help move the convicts into the main institution. As many as 500 from the Medium Security prison, the farm, the dairy and the Pueblo honor farm would have to be moved. Carrel, Captain Russ DeSalvo and the Patrol Squad met at the Fremont Airport where I briefed them on the physical layout of Medium Security and my plan for busing the convicts back to Old Max. Backed by the patrol squad, I was scheduled to confront the mob of rebellious inmates at 2:00 p.m. My order was, "No shooting unless they tried to climb over the fence or continued to violently resist after being ordered to the waiting buses."

At exactly 2:00 p.m. I confronted the rebels. The mob gathered around me, and one of the leaders, a very tough Hispanic, came up to me and asked, "Warden, are you going to move us inside?

"Yes sir, Jack," I replied. We were eye to eye.

"With guns?"

"Yes, with guns," I answered. "Look behind you and see the guns." He looked, but no guns. The patrol squad was just coming in the back gate.*

---

* I joked with Captain DeSalvo for many years thereafter. I accused the Squad of being so scared that they all had to go to the restroom before they could face the convicts.

The big Hispanic leader of the prisoners then said, "I'm done, Warden. What do you want me to do?"

"Step inside the door and take off your clothes for a strip search and then go get in the bus," I answered. He went to the doorway for the shakedown, and everyone started to follow.

"Bones,"* another one of the leaders, said, "Just point out the way. I'm not about to die with this crowd."

A small, black convict who weighed about ninety pounds was carrying a baseball bat, wearing a football helmet and running around trying to get everyone to resist. However, he soon decided he would be alone, so he melted into the defeated group and disappeared into a bus.

The media was able to take a few photos as the prison buses entered the gates at Old Max, and the convicts gave them a good show, waving fists and shouting. Although the media was upset that they had not been allowed to cover and photograph the roundup, all of the staff that had participated or drove the buses gave interviews which appeased them somewhat. One television group from KLZ did some sidewalk interviews, asking the citizenry if they were fearful of the breakout of convicts. It seemed no one was.

We now had the cell houses doubled up with a mass of howling, threatening, cursing convicts. (Some were even beginning to beg to have the whole thing called off.) Then the attorneys arrived, demanding to see their clients. Some were quite radical and said that they had heard that ten convicts and maybe more were marked for death. The attorneys threatened that dire consequences would befall me if they were not allowed to see the "marked" convicts and that these men were, in fact, injured or dead.

---

* When not in prison, "Bones" was leader of a biker group. Jack Cowperthwaite, the prison Business Manager, was driving one of the buses, and he always joked that I deliberately put "Bones" in his bus and seated him directly behind the driver's seat.

I responded by telling about ten or twelve attorneys that they could communicate in writing with their clients, and that I would guarantee delivery of the missives and give the clients the means to respond. The attorneys did not accept this edict and threatened to get a court order to make me allow them in to see their clients. "Do whatever you have to do," I told them, "but no one will be allowed to talk with clients until this upheaval is over!" (At that time the warden had huge, lawful powers to deal with insurrections, and I used them all.)

On the sixth day, Kostal, one of the convict leaders, sent word by a classification officer that if I would let him confer with about thirty other convicts, he could get the rebellion ended. Immediately, I went in to see him, and we had a long conversation.

"It looks like you big boys have run out of your stock of canteen grub and are getting hungry," I said. "We are still feeding some of the victims, and so I may open up and let the poor guys who wanted no part of this trouble go back to normal. I'll let you hard cases have a few more days of lockdown on me."

Kostal grinned but admitted nothing. Then I called Deputy Wyse and told him to assign someone to take the leader wherever he wished to go but to monitor all conversations and record whom he conferred with.

The following day we announced that the mutiny was over, and we started feeding in the dining room – one tier at a time – and I appointed a group to classify and consign each prisoner to either his old job or a reassignment to a new area. Not many who had been assigned previously to Medium Security or other outside facilities were allowed to return. The prison returned to its regular routine. The insurrection was over with only one injury – *a convict had a small cut on his wrist*!

Later, we were visited by a large number of prison personnel and wardens from around the country who wanted to study our methods of settling the uprising. We were even visited by the Commissioner of Prisons from Kenya, Africa. He was shocked that, during the tour, I talked with a large number of prisoners. He indicated that in Kenya (1967) they did not speak to prisoners during any inspection or tour of officials. His system had executed 39 persons in the previous six months, and he chuckled when I told him that we had executed one. He stated that they might do 39 more before the year's end.

Kenyan official (left) visits Warden Patterson
after the Insurrection of 1971.

Well, It's All Yours, Fred.

INTERPRETER / Jan-Feb '72

*I had just announced my retirement in February of 1972,
when this cartoon appeared in the "The Interpreter,"
the magazine produced by the convicts. Fred Wyse
was the Deputy Warden who would later become
Acting Warden. The serious disturbance in
November of 1971 resulted in considerable
property damage, but no one was killed
or seriously injured.*

*Convict Mike Coy drew this cartoon of Fred and me
and it caused a lot of laughs.*

– W.K.P.

178

Photos
from the
Insurrection
of November, 1971

As the saying goes, "A chain is no stronger than its weakest link," and there was not a weak link in our organization during the test which we went through last November. I am delighted that the staff is made up of people of this caliber, people who are there when and where needed, with no thought to time or regularly assigned duties.

*— Wayne K. Patterson,
following the Insurrection of November 1971*

*Officers making thousands of sandwiches
and getting eggs ready for the daily feeding of inmates.*

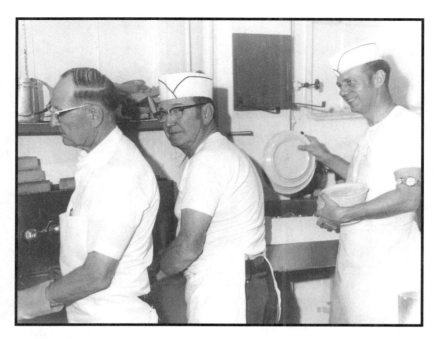

Dishwashing, an endless chore for officers during the disturbance.

*Patterson (center) with officers
who took on "kitchen duty" during insurrection.*

Officers in the new trade of "meat cutters."

Officers making wooden windows to replace broken glass.

Officer Stumph, baker during the disturbance.
It was said that he made great pies!

Note psychology text (upper left) amid litter tossed from cells.

Feeding inmates in dining hall at the end of the insurretion of 1971.

Officers distributing prescription medications.

An inmate left a note on his cell making his lunch wishes known.

Those Who Keep the Keys

MY MARY

Behind every successful man there stands a
woman of talent and virtue.

—unknown

There are many unforgettable
sagas of the men and
women who filled the cells and
bunks of the prisons of another
era, and of their keepers. There
are stories of corollary actors
who played well-remembered
roles during my forty years in
some type of law enforcement.
However, no story exceeded
that of Miss Mary, my "pardner"
during all of those years.

Mary came from a
family of ten who were working
hard to survive the great
depression of the thirties. I first
met her in July 1939, and we fell
in love – at first sight. We married in November, and from then on
it was like the Biblical story of Ruth – "Whither thou goest, I will
go; and where thou lodgest, I will lodge." Moves for my career
took us from Steamboat Springs to Denver to Limon, back to
Denver to Buena Vista to Canon, back to Denver and finally to
Cañon City again. During these moves my Mary bore and reared

189

two children, Monte (who entered the Marine Corps and later became a Denver policeman) and Tammy, (reared on the grounds of two prisons who became a mother and later a career woman.)

My Mary had the ability to adjust to any type of daily life that my career dictated, and it was often quite diverse. We went through some tough times in 1941 when I was appointed on the State Patrol at a salary of $105 per month, and we had an eighteen-month-old baby boy. Mary managed the budget, and we always made it from one month to another. We were paid on the fifth and the twentieth of the month, and sometimes creditors would call on the first of the month and threaten. Patiently, Mary told them of the paydays, but the next month brought the same pressure. We would sometimes laugh and say, "They can't put us in jail for slow pay."

Transferred from Limon to Denver, I got lucky and was appointed by Governor Ralph Carr as his driver and bodyguard – no more money but a huge jump in public recognition. When I was drafted into the military during World War II, Mary was left with our son Monte. I drew $56 a month in the Navy, and she got a small allowance. She took this turn of events with her usual pragmatism. I had learned a bit of Spanish in school, and I affectionately called her "La Senora Maria con mucho trabajo y dinero poco." (the lady Mary with much work and little money).

After the war, I was appointed to the State Civil Service Commission for four years, followed by a seven-year appointment to the State Department of Parole. Eventually, I became Warden at two penal institutions.

We were the last warden's family to live on the grounds at Buena Vista, as well as the last family to live on the grounds of the prison at Cañon City. Mary was always the strong glue that held my career and the children's education on an even keel. She took charge of a house and grounds manned by convicts. Outside of her family, the key persons in her daily life were the inmates – the housemen, the cooks and the convict at the garage. Although the grounds personnel were supervised by an officer, Mary often directed the planting of flower beds and the greenhouse.

Mary hosted governors, legislators and other public officials and guests. This involved her planning every meal, ordering all household supplies and supervising approximately fourteen convicts each day. Mary was always very careful to obey the security rules and always treated the prisoners as just ordinary people, regardless of their crimes that had brought them to prison. The prisoners were all very protective of her and Tammy and were very respectful.

However, once Mary was nearly taken hostage but was saved by our dog, Joe T. The Buena Vista institution was not completely secure as a roadway wound through the grounds and no gates were manned. Mary had backed her car from the garage and returned to the garage for some reason, leaving the driver's door ajar. Joe T. always considered an open car an invitation to go for a ride, so he headed for the auto just as Mary returned. In the meantime, on the other side of the car, a tall young Hispanic prisoner was planning to join Mary as she left the prison. Seemingly the man appeared from nowhere and grabbed the door handle. *He and Joe T. met eye to eye!* The prisoner blinked, backed away from the car and hurried back to his work gang. He said later that he was new at working outside the walls and thought it would be a good chance to escape* but that "the police dog scared me away." (Actually, the convict didn't know how *safe* he was as Joe T. was fairly harmless and seemed to love all prisoners.)

Still, this incident did not seem to make Mary afraid as she was always too busy with her family and her duties as the

---

*The next day this prisoner escaped and, after stealing a car and running it out of gas, was captured the next evening walking along Texas Creek approximately seventeen miles from the prison. Ten years later this convict studied for and was ordained a minister.

warden's wife. She hosted piano recitals for Tammy and her young friends, was a Den Mother for Cub Scouts, entertained her friends at bridge, hosted parties at holidays and attended events – all inside the prison. She endured publicity – both good and bad. In short, Miss Mary made my entire career a reality!

HERE COMES THE BREEZE

by John Mullenix

NOTE: Every second or third day I entered the prison from my home through the west gate and looked over the prison to see if there were any problems. If nothing urgent came to my attention, I spent a couple of hours inside the compound. This story about me was written as a school project by Mullenix, a hardcore escape artist. He escaped once from Cañon City but was caught immediately. He was there when I left as Warden, but escaped once again in 1973. Ten months later, he was arrested for bank robbery in Seattle, found guilty and sentenced to a federal prison. The paper is presented here without any editing.

–W.K.P.

From the library to the far corner of the sandstone mess-hall the most addle-brained surveyor in the world could measure at most a distance of about one-hundred yards. Walking a definitely-indefinite pattern, my senile sauce-sipping granny could cover it completely blasted in an easy three to four minutes. Yet–here's a fiftyish bear like of a con-man knocking it out in about four hours and some odd change.

Whoever the convict, it is apparent he owned a keen sense of characterization when he hung the "cool breeze" handle on Warden Patterson. The guy comes on about as shook-up as Kleenex. Whether it's grass, goof-balls or clean living he's coasting on, that half-smile and little boy's grin never leaves his blue eyes and pink cherubic face.

From his unscheduled entrance at the west gate until he slowly fades beyond the far corner of the mess-hall, his Santa Claus eyes remain at work. No definite business-like answers this guy. He uses two tools only in smoothing the feathers on the problems of the endlessly hovering cons. He listens, he smiles. Give him a pipe to add to the conservative yet casual attire, the neat grey hair, and you'd have the father-doctor-dean-lawyer profile complete.

It's about three easy strides from the gate when the first cat pulls him over and whips his story on him. As he hesitates to listen and mollify, the grape vine goes into action. Like out of the wood-work the problem bearing types begin gliding in to intercept.

Each time he makes this scene, he draws a typical group....like some real brown-nose of a drip doing about 33 more days, a jail-house polititian [sic] or two, guys asking for good time, conjugal visits etc....even a hard nosed con once in a while. About two sidewalk interviews per ten yards I'd venture to say.

Really now...! four hours to make the hundred yards? It seems to me that such an important state official could better utilize his time....like getting my holds dropped, or getting me better working conditions on this lousy job I have. In fact, I think I'll tell him so the next time I see him come through here.

Mullenix's escape while I was the Warden occurred during a big snow storm. He and the four other escapees were captured immediately, December 15, 1967.

In the 1973 escape (after I had left the institution), Mullenix took as hostage at knife point officer Rocky Canda, supervisor of athletics and the gymnasium. Fortunately, he released the officer unharmed in Colorado Springs.

Prior to his appearance in Colorado, Mullenix and several other prisoners had tunneled under the wall at the Walla Walla prison in Washington. Although he was an affable man, he was a hard core convict leader and always an escape risk.

Chairman of Corrections Harry Tinsley,
Retired Warden Clinton Duffy of San Quentin Prison,
and Warden Wayne Patterson
at a conference on the
1966 Colorado Death Penalty Referendum.

RHODES VS. PATTERSON
U. S. District Court, District of Colorado

A book might be written on the injustice of the just.
- Anthony Hope

In a period of 40 years as an executive in government, you become somewhat "case hardened" to lawsuits with your name as the defendant. If memory serves me well, I was named in 190 lawsuits. Some were frightening, with the plaintiff demanding millions in punitive damages.* My salary at that time as Warden was $24,000 a year.

Other lawsuits were not so frightening as they only demanded that I do some service. For example, I was sued because the prison didn't serve a good brand of peanut butter. I resisted but have always thought that if I hadn't been so bullheaded and had ordered that "Skippy" be served, the judge would have dismissed the case. I considered my administration "a beneficent dictatorship" and felt that I was in the forefront of prison modernization at that time – so the lawsuits offended me.

During the outside protests of the 1960s, the inside convict activists followed the trend and elicited the services of the ACLU, radical lawyers and "jailhouse" lawyers to pour hundreds of lawsuits into the state and federal courts. The prisons were

---

* I believe I was the first warden in the United States to be sued in excess of one million dollars; however it became a common practice after that.

perceived by protestors and activists as places where a corrupt government could control and frustrate dissidents.

The Federal courts, which previously had a historic hands off policy in regard to prison management, began "full press" forward into prison management. Some courts actually micro-managed some prisons in the U.S. by appointing monitors to enforce court orders. The agitating convict activists began to see the Federal courts as their advocates, not as arbitrators.

From 1968 until I retired in 1972, I was named defendant in all sorts of lawsuits. They included:

- a rule against beards, mustaches and long hair
- toilet paper being too harsh
- poor peanut butter
- not having a complete law library for the use of convict lawyers to challenge their conviction
- inadequate health care – or health care not of the prisoner's choice
- no legal representation or due process in disciplinary hearings
- ill fitting false teeth
- inadequate denture prosthesis
- not having inmates' personal physicians tend them at public expense
- unconstitutional conditions in the disciplinary section of the prison - "cruel and unusual punishment"
- no religious diets (serving pork, for example)
- not allowing "sweat lodges"
- depriving prisoners of their rights under color of authority

The lawsuits went on and on *ad infinitum.* However, the strangest case that I had was *Rhodes vs. Patterson, et. al.,* where the plaintiff reached out from the grave to get millions — *millions that I didn't have*. The case continued long after I had retired and took on other named defendants, but the demands remained.

Laurence Rhodes (#36628) was received at the prison in March 1965. As was my practice I went to the intake unit every Friday to interview any new arrivals. I found Rhodes in his cell and saw on my note pad that he was to serve a life sentence for the murder of a young girl in Jefferson County. He was twenty-two years old, of medium build, had blonde hair and bright blue eyes which peered directly at me. I noted that he looked pretty wild, but that was not unusual for new prisoners.

About a year or so later I met Rhodes during my rounds of the compound and inquired of his activities. Immediately, he launched into a long story about his playing basketball in the big yard. During that exercise he had injured his back. Then he listed some complaints for which Dr. Ralston (the prison doctor) had prescribed a brace and some pills that Rhodes felt hadn't helped. I told him I would speak with the doctor.

When I returned to the office, I checked his record and noticed that Rhodes was the editor of *The Clarion*, the Saint Dismas Holy Name Society's publication in the prison. I called the prison chaplain, Father Justin, and he said that Rhodes was very active and seemed very sincere in his religious beliefs.

Then I spoke with Dr. Ralston who indicated that he felt Rhodes had some mental problems. He told me, "Rhodes can't face up to the life sentence, and he plans to take any means possible to avoid it."

Dr. George Levy, the prison psychologist agreed. "He's a strange case and may need some psychological help. I'll refer him to the psychiatric team from the State Hospital the next time they are here." Since the medical staff was in contact with Rhodes, I forgot about the complaint and tended to what I felt was more urgent prison business.

Sometime thereafter, Deputy Warden Fred Wyse came into my office to report, "Rhodes made a botched attempt at suicide last night – drank some caustic fluid of some kind and tried to cut his throat. The doctor says he'll live but should be evaluated by the mental hospital. The doctors (Ralston and Levy) recommend that he be transferred to the State Hospital."

Rhodes was transferred and shortly thereafter the mental hospital sent me a recommendation that he remain for treatment for both his mental and physical problems. Following our usual procedure, I advised the hospital that Rhodes was serving a life sentence and was considered a *high risk* for escape.

Several months later, Deputy Wyse again gave me a report on Rhodes. "Captain Russell DeSalvo of the State Patrol called and said the patrol had stopped a car on U.S. 96 in the mountains. The occupants were two nurses from the State Hospital, another male patient and life-termer Laurence Rhodes. Captain DeSalvo said that it 'looked like a big romance, but the trooper sent them back to the hospital after checking them out.'"

I called the hospital and received no satisfactory reason for Rhodes being away from the institution. However, one individual informed me that Rhodes had "off-grounds privileges as a part of his treatment program." After burning a few ears at the hospital, I ordered that Rhodes be returned to the prison. At that time the commitment *mittimus* stated that prisoners were "committed to the custody of the Warden," and I could see large headlines as a result of this "off-grounds privilege" for a murderer under a life sentence.

Immediately after his return to the prison Rhodes wrote me several letters complaining of his lack of treatment and demanding to be returned to the mental hospital. Finally, I told him that his medical treatment was going to be administered by the prison medical staff unless it required a service that our medical staff could not provide. He secured an attorney and sued.

The lawsuit – that continued for 11 years – detailed a history of suffering from the original injury with no medical attention and, in strong legal terms, accused me, the Deputy, the three prison doctors, the Governor, etc. I retired in 1972 but remained a principal defendant.

Apparently, Governor Vanderhoof, at the urging of Rhodes' girlfriend and his attorney, commuted his sentence in 1973 and allowed his release on parole. Rhodes married his girlfriend, and my only contact was when a new suit was filed and accepted by the court. I was called in the "discovery" aspects of the suit and the pretrial statements entered by the attorney in our (the defendants) behalf. On February 6, 1976, I received a letter from the Assistant Attorney General, who was representing the Deputy Warden and me. (I had now been retired as Warden for four years.) The letter contained two shocking paragraphs – at least shocking to me.

> The primary factor responsible for the lengthy delay in getting this case resolved is that Mr. Rhodes was fatally shot by his wife in October 1974. Upon learning of his death we anticipated that the litigation would not be pursued. The original attorney moved to withdraw from the case and was permitted to do so. The wife, who was questioned by the Grand Jury and released without being charged, was permitted by the Federal Court to become the plaintiff and sue on behalf of the estate of Mr. Rhodes The attorney for the plaintiff has now submitted to us a list of potential witnesses which he plans to call at the time of trial…

> Generally speaking the plaintiff's counsel states that these individuals will testify to either the inadequacy or the complete refusal of the defendants to treat and prescribe medication for the plaintiff. On the face of it, it does not appear to me that any of these witnesses can testify that any of the prison officials knew or should

have known that the defendant was being deprived of his civil rights by the lack of treatment given by the prison physicians. . .

The suit sought $2 million for four claims for relief and $2 million as punitive damages, plus attorney fees and costs. There was also a demand for a trial by a jury of twelve. The longer the case went on – I was still responding to the case in 1976 – and with no access to prison records, I began to believe *my life savings were going to be given to a dead man and, from his grave, to his killer!*

However, my luck held, and after several more years of legal wrangling, the case was dismissed. Sometimes I think ulcers and heart attacks could kill off a warden who considers himself a just and caring man.

FREDDY AND "THE MILLION-DOLLAR HAIRCUT"

*Someone made and recorded a sort of institute and digest
of anarchy called the rights of man.*

                                                          -Burke

During the 1960s and the early 1970s there was strong legal
effort by prisoners to alter their sentences and conditions of
their confinement. Suits of all types were filed in both state and
federal courts. (See *Rhodes vs Patterson.*) There were times when
I thought I was being drowned in a sea of legalism as the warden
was always named "the keeper" in ninety percent of the suits. I
was named the defendant in the first million-dollar prison lawsuit
in the United States. After that, of course, a million dollars became
a mere pittance as the prisoner suits demanded more and more
money.

A MILLION DOLLARS!! It became a bit frightening when
the suits demanded personal liability as well as liability connected
with my official duties, and I could see all of my life savings slipping
away. Fortunately, I was defended by competent attorneys from the
State Attorney General's office, but it was still scary.

I called other wardens around the country and found that
their prisoner's legal demands were to correct perceived injustices
such as conjugal visits, better peanut butter or softer toilet paper.
My lawsuit was about beards, mustaches and long hair. After

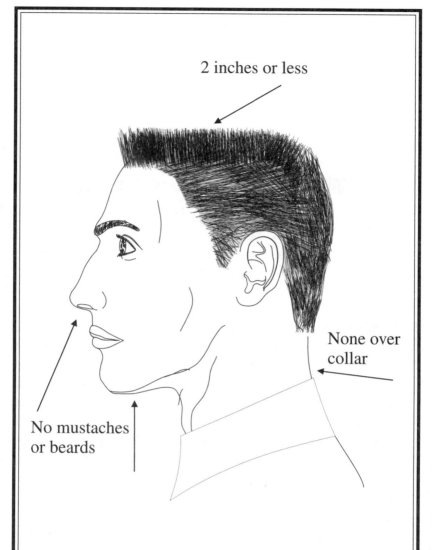

2 inches or less

None over collar

No mustaches or beards

"Mug shots" used for identification were taken after the prisoner was bathed, deloused, had hair cut off and prison clothing issued.

A drawing similar to this was posted in all areas where barbering was done.

reading the lawsuit several times, it appeared to me that I was violating the "Treaty of Guadalupe-Hidalgo" wherein Hispanic men were to wear long hair and beards to demonstrate their macho personalities. Neither my attorney nor I was familiar with the "Treaty."

The rule that precipitated the suit was that all prisoners were required to be clean shaven at all times and hair was to be no longer than two inches long at the top with both ears showing and no hair hanging down over the collar. The rule had been in existence at the prison for many years, and a detailed drawing was available showing the specified appearance. I had reviewed the rule since, during that period of time, men in society outside the prison were beginning to sport beards and long hair.

My decision to continue the rule differed from other prisons in that our internal control was predicated on the ability of prisoners to manufacture curios (with tools in their cells) in their spare time. The result was that we were escorting 30,000 to 40,000 tourists through the prison annually, and another 4,000 to 5,000 were entering the prison to participate in religious services, Alcoholics Anonymous and other group meetings. It appeared that security could be a problem, and it had been breached by a bearded, long-haired inmate melting in with the visitors as they exited the prison. In addition, the kitchen and dining room was manned with inmates, and we found that other inmates resented the long-haired, bearded prisoners cooking and serving their food. I decided that the rule must stay – and be enforced.

Calm prevailed until one day I saw Freddy in the Big Yard chatting with his friends and wearing long hair and a goatee. I said, "Freddy, get your hair cut and get a shave."

Freddy made no response, but since my word was law in those days, I put him out of my mind and went to other business. About a week later I again saw Freddy, and he had another week's growth of hair and goatee. I could see that he had a large audience, so I ordered him to accompany me to the barber chair in cell house three. Once there, I cut his hair and, using the same clippers, I took off his goatee. I also left him for ten days in isolation.

Nearly a month later I saw Freddy with his hair and beard adhering to the rule. Shortly thereafter I was served with lawsuit demanding $1,000,000–$500,000 exemplary damages, $500,000 for punitive damages, plus all lawyer's fees. The document nearly burned my fingers, and I quickly sent it to the Attorney General.

After a period of legal exchanges, we went to trial in Federal Court in Denver. The judge was from Oklahoma, sitting in the Denver court. For two days the trial continued, with Freddy as the only witness. There were moments of humor when Freddy stated, "Warden Patterson gave me a 'whitewall' while two other inmates held me in the barber's chair. He singled me out for punishment while there were other prisoners with long hair."

The judge interrupted, "What's a 'whitewall'?"

"He skinned all the hair off my head and left me bald," Freddy explained morosely.

My attorneys presented the written rule with the descriptive drawing and the reasons the rule was in existence. Suddenly, the judge concluded the hearing and removed a load from my back.

"There will be no finding for the complainant in this court," the judge declared. "The rule is reasonable, and if the warden hasn't caught all the rule violators, I'm confident that he will – shortly. The case is dismissed."

However, the victory in the case was an empty one for after I retired all personal appearance rules were abolished and long hair and facial hair became standard. At the same time all tours of the prison were discontinued.

Lawsuits became a way of life for prison administrators. For example, I was named a defendant in 142 filings during 1972.

– W.K.P

THE KEEPER LOSES HIS KEY

Psychology as practiced in a prison setting
has no textbook or guidelines and may be animalistic.
-WKP

Roberto, a short, heavyset, fifteen-year-old orphan who came to the Buena Vista Reformatory in the 1950s from the San Luis Valley. Coal black hair that grew low on his forehead was swept back to his neckline, and sparkling black eyes seemed to radiate good humor. He was probably the most "streetwise" person that I ever supervised, considering his young age. Immediately, he became a leader of the Hispanics who numbered nearly half of the Buena Vista facility census at that time.

Roberto was always very respectful, calling me Warden "Potterson" and Deputy Warden Carl Douglas, Mr. "Dooglus." Mr. Douglas opined that Roberto "don't have much to think with." Nothing was further from the truth as subsequent activities seemed to prove. He was a master at out-thinking his keepers but later succumbed to the primitive psychology of his prison training.

The warden's residence on the grounds of the Buena Vista institution was an ancient two-story building that had been built in the late 1880s and had been designed as a barracks for unmarried officers. It had been remodeled over the years and contained a living room, dining room, large kitchen, sun porch

Old warden's residence at Buena Vista. Built in 1880s as an officers barracks, it was razed in 1962. On the left is visitor Kibby Gart of Gart Bros. with Wayne K. Patterson in 1959.

and six upstairs bedrooms. Staff for the residence were all convicts and consisted of a cook, a waiter who was also assistant housekeeper, a housekeeper and ten grounds keepers. In addition, there were also six convicts living in a bunkhouse behind the residence who worked outside the "security perimeter." Roberto had finally been able to acquire an outside job working on the lawn and by diligent work and "conning" the supervising officer, he was allowed to live in the bunkhouse. I took a jaundiced view of this convict's new found freedom but did not reverse the supervisor's decision.

In 1956, my son Monte had enlisted in the Marine Corps, so had never moved into the residence with the rest of the family. However, he had left his 1950 Ford auto stored in a small, unused garage on the grounds. Doors of the garage were seldom opened except occasionally by maintenance personnel. One day while Mary and I were in Denver, my daughter Tammy (who was staying with the Douglases on the Reformatory grounds) got off the school bus and saw that the garage door was open and Monte's car was gone. She told Deputy Douglas, who investigated and called me in Denver to report that the car was missing along with Roberto and our cook, a check-writing convict named Fleckinger.

That was not all that was missing! When Mary and I arrived home, we found that my clothes closet had been ransacked. Two pair of slacks, an expensive sport coat and a pair of my shoes had disappeared. In the pocket of my sport coat was a large flat BRASS KEY which would allow me to go through any *inside* door in the prison – cellblocks, dormitories, kitchen – but, fortunately, would *not open any outside* door. After assessing the security hazards of the purloined key, I decided that the security of the institution was not compromised, although the recovery of the key was of utmost importance for in the hands of a prisoner it could cause disaster. *We must capture Roberto and find the missing KEY!*

Immediately, I ordered a state-wide alert with descriptions of the two men, and the next day I was rewarded with the news that Fleckinger had been captured in Montrose, Colorado. Roberto had been spotted in the willows along the Uncompaghre River, north of Montrose. I made a check of the ex-prisoners living in the Montrose area and obtained their addresses from the parole office. Then I drove to Montrose, checked with the Sheriff and other officers on the hunt, visited the county jail and talked to the ex-cook, Fleckinger. He knew little except that he and Roberto had abandoned the getaway car in an empty garage in Leadville and had parted company.

Next, I went to the home of the first ex-prisoner on my list, a two-time loser named Sandy C. He invited me in and introduced me to his wife and child.

"I'm looking for Roberto, Sandy. I know you and he were pals in prison. Have you seen him?"

"No, Warden," Sandy was quick to reply. "I haven't seen him, and I didn't know he had escaped."

I talked to Sandy for over an hour, and he swore he knew nothing. However, as I stood up to thank Sandy and take my leave, I noticed *SANDY WAS WEARING MY SHOES – MY NUNN-BUSH OXFORDS!!*

We sat back down and after some urging and a couple of threats, Sandy admitted that he had let Roberto stay there for the night. Sandy was pretty shaky as he could see cell doors closing behind him again.

"I paid Roberto two dollars for the shoes, Warden," Sandy explained, nervously rubbing his hands together, "but I didn't know the shoes were yours. I know nothing about the other clothes though."

Finally, I awarded the shoes to Sandy and left. That evening Roberto finally was captured, wet and tired, walking in the bottoms by the river. Both escapees were returned "home" and spent a few days in isolation on a restricted diet of bread and spinach. However, there was still the problem of the missing *KEY*. It had to be found!

Several days later I learned that officers were unable to locate my son's car in Leadville, so I decided to try my luck at finding the stolen auto. Deputy Douglas and I got Roberto and put him in the back of the deputy's car.

"Roberto," I said, "We want you to take us to the car you stole – *and I want that KEY!*"

"Warden Potterson, I can take you to the car in Leadville," Roberto responded, "but I hitched a ride to Montrose and threw the key out the window of that car."

"O.K., Roberto," I said. "We are going to help your memory, and we don't want to spend a lot of time listening to you lie. *I want the car and the key, and you are going to produce both!*"

A long silence ensued while Roberto digested this conversation. Eventually we reached Leadville, and Roberto directed us through some side streets and to an old, empty garage behind a vacant house where the pair had hidden Monte's car. It had been cross wired and was out of gas but had no other damage. (I called on the radio and had it driven home.)

"Now, Roberto, what did you do with my clothes?"

Roberto didn't respond to the question, and we continued driving until we rounded a corner where Roberto suddenly called out, "Stop here! I'll get them for you." He walked up to a big trash can and pulled out two pair of pants.

As I stared at the wrinkled clothing, I couldn't figure out why the two convicts had taken them. I was six foot one and weighed 220 pounds. Roberto was about five foot four and weighed approximately 145 pounds.

"Roberto, what was on your mind to steal my clothes?" I asked in a puzzled voice. "Fleckinger is smaller than you, and neither of you could wear the garments."

"I figured we could trade or pawn them," Roberto explained, looking somewhat sheepish.

"Well, I gave the shoes to Sandy that you sold him," I said, emphasizing the word *sold*.

"I gave him the shoes, not sold them. For a night at his house and some food. They fit him real good." Roberto was now affable and grinning.

Shaking my head, I asked, "Where is my coat? I don't see my coat."

"I gave it to the man that gave me the ride – for five dollars," Roberto added. He seemed rather pleased with himself at the bargain he had made, and I began to think we were involved in a Laurel and Hardy comedy situation.

"Now, Roberto," I said in a stern voice to impress him with the seriousness of the situation, "we are going to take the highway between here and Red Cliff, and you will show us where you threw the key out."

"I don't know! I don't know." The change in my attitude had Roberto more concerned about what I would do if we could not find the key. "I'll try, but I don't know."

Deputy Douglas and I drove slowly over Battle Mountain with Roberto looking out the car window to find the spot where he had tossed the missing item. There were long periods of silence as we drove up the pass, but I was convinced that Roberto's mind was working on some solution to get himself out of the problem. Finally he called out, "Maybe here!"

The three of us wearily crawled from the car and searched the barrow pit and a small gully with no results. We also searched about ten other spots with no luck. I believed that Roberto knew where the key was but decided not to go on to Red Cliff at that time. As we drove back down Battle Mountain, I told Roberto to keep looking as we were going to find that key. However, I had the feeling that Roberto had decided not to take my warning seriously.

At the bottom of the pass, near the Eagle River, we drove off the road into a large grassy area and stopped beside a picnic table. After another period of questioning Roberto, I decided to test a bit of prison psychology on this well-calcified psychopath. Some may think my tactics harsh or cruel. Maybe, but this con man was not going to reveal where the key was, and if the key made its way to some of his prison friends, I worried that it could cost the lives of both officers and other convicts at the prison.

"Mr. Douglas," I said in a stage whisper as I leaned over to the Deputy's ear, "have you got your gun with you?"

"Sure, I always have my gun."

"Do you have a shovel in the car?"

212

"Yep!" The Deputy replied, still whispering. "It's in the trunk."

Speaking in a slightly louder voice, as I knew Roberto was now listening intently to our conversation, I proposed a plan. "Doug, let's just kill this renegade right here and now and bury him. We can just say he escaped. He's nothing to anybody. He was a disappointment to his family, who abandoned him. The police in the valley won't spend much time looking for him. He thinks you and I are fools. The whole country will be happy if he is gone from the scene, and . . ." I let my words trail off.

"Warden Potterson. Warden Potterson," Roberto interrupted loudly. "If you will take me back up to Red Cliff, I think I can find the key."

"No, Roberto. We have wasted the day with you, and we have decided on a new program. We are going to forget the key. It's now noon. Mr. Douglas has a couple of sandwiches. We'll get out of the car, share them and then return to the prison."

"I ain't hungry, and I don't want to get out, Warden Potterson." Roberto was now quite agitated and made no move to leave the vehicle. "I'm now telling you the truth. If you take me to Red Cliff, I can fnd the key."

Mr. Douglas and I got out of the car and sat down at the picnic table. We had a lunch box with some sandwiches and a thermos of coffee. After we had eaten, Mr. Douglas went to the trunk of the car, removed a shovel and struck it into the ground by the table. We lingered in the tranquility of the tall spruce and pine trees with the murmur of the water the only sound around us. Finally, I said in a loud voice, "Deputy, I would like to be buried in a place like this myself."

From the car came a wail. "No! No! I don't want to stay here," Roberto protested, pushing himself into the far corner of the back seat. "Warden Potterson, I'm telling you the truth now. If you take me to Red Cliff, I can find the key. Get back in the car. Please get back in the car."

After several minutes of appearing to mull over what Roberto was asking, I finally said, "Well, I guess Mr. Douglas and I will give you one more chance, but unless you can produce that key, we will come back this way and stop here at this spot. You understand?"

Roberto nodded and smiled weakly. Relaxing a little, he stretched out his hand to the Deputy. "I guess I'll have a sandwich if there're any left, Mr. Dooglas."

We drove back over Battle Mountain to Red Cliff, stopped in an alley and made our way up to a second-floor apartment. Roberto rapped on the door, and a young male about twenty years of age answered. "Es el Jefe del encaro," Roberto explained as a number of other members of the family came to the door, all of them talking excitedly in Spanish. The children seemed frightened, and using my limited Spanish, I tried to reassure them that they were not in any trouble.

"Si, into the river," the young man answered when Roberto questioned him as to where they had tossed the key. He agreed to accompany us to search for the lost item.

Slowly we drove down the other side of Battle Mountain Pass from Red Cliff toward Minturn. When we arrived on a bridge over the river, the young man pointed toward the stream bed and Roberto agreed as to the site. "O.K.," I said, "produce the key."

The river was about two feet deep, roaring through a series of boulders and ice cold! Both men took off their shoes and socks, rolled up their trousers, waded into the water and felt around the boulders with their hands, which immediately became numb. I realized that we were punishing the young man who had tried to help a brethren out by driving Roberto to Minturn. The man had no criminal record and was cooperating with us, so I relented and told them both to come onto the bank. "Muchas gracias por el favor," I said to the young man, once again calling upon my limited Spanish.

Now I was convinced that this was the location of my KEY,

and I decided to discontinue the hunt. That bridge and that stretch of the Eagle River became the KEEPER OF THE KEY. I forgot to ask further about my missing coat, and I never saw it again.

Roberto, a master prison psychologist himself, was a victim of his own primitive instincts. I am certain that he truly believed that Deputy Douglas and I would kill and bury him and cover up the crime by saying that he had escaped. In a world of unbelievers, he was one of a kind. He lived to come to the prison several more times. Later, he killed a man in Española, New Mexico, and spent several years in the New Mexico Prison in Santa Fe. When I visited that prison one time, Roberto heard I was there and asked to see me. He merely wanted to talk for a few minutes, and when I asked him about the murder in Española, he explained the incident away as if it were only an accident. "Warden Potterson, it was just a fight, and he jumped onto my shank."*

In contacts with several thousand criminals during my career, Roberto was one of the most unforgettable, He was thoroughly at home in prison, fluent in two languages, a natural prison leader (particularly among the Hispanics). He had no visitors nor correspondents; yet he had contacts which he retained in both Colorado and New Mexico. When his followers in the prisons were released, he kept their addresses in small books hidden in his socks. He shuffled them around during shakedowns, but I recall officers collecting about ten books with over a hundred names.

If he is still alive, Roberto would be over seventy and probably still "conning" his way through trouble. He would have been a criminologist's dream for a chapter in a textbook. Certainly, he was a part of *my* "hands-on education" of criminal behavior.

---

* See Glossary.

*Warden Roy Patterson talking with
James "Mad Dog" Sherbondy in Little Siberia.
Denver Police characterized Sherbondy
as the most dangerous juvenile the department
ever dealt with. Sherbody was the ringleader
of the 1947 prison break featured in the story,
"Last Days of a Troubled Life."*

REMEMBERING
THOSE WHO KEPT THE KEYS

In all prisons, there are those people who spend their days "keeping an eye" on the people whom society has sentenced to time behind the walls. The Warden of my day was a very powerful administrator. The Governor and Director of Institutions were the only supervisors, with a Chief of Corrections for liaison. However, the law gave all of the authority to the Warden.

Cary Stiff, a *Denver Post* reporter at that time wrote:

The prison Warden heads a most complex social institution. He must be an educator heading the prison's rudimentary school system. He bosses the prison hospital. He runs the prison industries, which include everything from a hog farm to a slaughter house, license place factory to a cannery, barbershop to a soap factory. As the prison's top administrator, he is responsible for the increasingly important task of classifying prisoners according to their background and needs. He supervises the prison's annual budget request – and he must convince the legislature to grant his requests. As the top management man at the penitentiary he must deal with the demands of the guards' union. He must be extremely adept at public relations. He has police powers and *de facto* judicial powers. He runs a completely self-contained "city" about the size of Julesburg, Colorado – with far more clout than the Mayor of Julesburg every dreamed of having.

As administrators of a correctional institution, individuals can *lead public opinion* as long as they don't get *too far ahead*, and they can *follow public opinion* as long as they don't *follow too far behind*. If they fail in either of these categories, they are prime candidates to become history as the public will find some way to replace them.

Of course, the Warden can set prison policy* but cannot run the prison without the able help of the staff. He must delegate authority to commanders to enforce rules and preserve order in the institution and authorize these individuals to take action that may mean life or death to subordinates or prisoners. This was the law at that time – an awesome responsibility.

Those who elect to work in a prison setting must always be aware of the possibility for violence. This cannot be completely controlled. There are many inmates that are violence-prone, and when people are confined in close quarters, under regimentation, a psychosis is induced with an attendant propensity for violence. As an example, there was an inmate who one morning killed his next cell neighbor with a homemade "shank." When I asked him what had happened to cause this, he explained, "The bastard kept flushing his toilet all night, and when he lined up in front of me to go to breakfast, I hit him."

Prior to 1954 there had been little training for newly hired officers in Cañon City. An officer who came to work in the cell houses was handed keys and told, "The convict tier runner can tell you what needs to be done." Later on, after initial classroom

---

* See Appendix for the "Orientation Lecture to the New Incoming Prisoners" which was given to all convicts entering the penitentiary.

training officers were required to walk three shifts with a training officer. Some were assigned to the towers on a seniority basis and stayed there until there was a ground vacancy. During my time the problem was that if everyone stayed on the job and there were no turnovers, a young, able officer could be trapped in the seniority system. I tried some alternatives but morale seemed to deteriorate, so the old system was reinstated. Of course, some preferred the towers, and that was helpful. One officer retired while I was there, and he had worked the same west gate tower for thirty-five years.

In my opinion, it takes a special kind of individual to accept the challenge of working with those incarcerated. During my time in the corrections field, I have met and worked with many exceptional men and women. They were loyal, hardworking professional people, but there is not room in this book to name all of them. Below are brief remembrances of merely a few of these individuals.

Harry Tinsley

Harry Tinsley and I came along in the penal system at about the same time. He was Deputy Warden at Buena Vista, when I was driver and bodyguard for Governors Carr and Vivian. We were friends and confidants for over thirty years. He became Acting Warden during the suspension of Roy Best and then Warden, after Roy's death in 1954. Harry was a kind man, and many people thought he was too nice to be a warden since those holding that position had been conditioned to the "rough and tough" 20-years of the Roy Best era.

Harry was successful in changing the course of Colorado prison history. As an educator by vocation, he introduced many educational reforms into the prison system. He enjoyed working with younger inmates and always tried to provide a program that would benefit the younger prisoner, particularly in the education area. In addition, he started the first

Two Wardens
Wayne K. Patteron (left) and Harry Tinsley (right).

classification of prisoners according to their background, needs and criminal sophistication. He also encouraged the longtime "hard cases" to mend their ways and helped them to get a chance at freedom.

Although Harry was opposed to the death penalty, he was required to officiate at seven executions and was a witness at one other. Because of his strong personal feelings about executions, he suffered after each was carried out.

He finally retired as Chief of Corrections where he was a great supporter of mine, working as liaison with the Director of the Department of Institutions and with the governor. Harry Tinsley was also well-known across the country and held many national offices in the corrections area.

Carl Douglas and Lovell Gentry

Two of the best "inside men" that I worked with during my time were Carl Douglas and Lowell Gentry. Douglas was Deputy Warden at the Buena Vista facility while I was there as Warden and later was Associate Warden at the Medium Security Prison while I was Warden at that facility. He was a big man, barrel-chested with big hands, a product of

Carl Douglas

Mountain Home, Arkansas, where he was born and spent his early life.

Douglas had a knack for understanding young men, and he always seemed to know everything that was happening in the institution. He did the final interview when inmates were assigned outside "the main" – to the farm or dairy. Later, we developed a classification group to make recommendation, and Deputy Douglas was the final word, subject only to my veto which I seldom used.

I had gone to Buena Vista during a severe riot and was appointed Warden a short time later. After the uprising, the institution was destabilized for a lengthy period of time thereafter, and Deputy Douglas was a big help in restoring order.

One night I was awakened at 1:00 a.m. by a call from the Night Captain. "Warden," he began, "there are four or five inmates armed with knives* loose in the institution. They have

---

* Later it was determined that the "knives" were a ring of keys.

been in "A" block, and we think they may have gotten out of Isolation and have keys."

I dressed, hurried to the entrance and met Deputy Douglas who also had been called. We had no weapons, but I was depending on some gas guns in a vault in the Captain's office. Deputy Douglas grabbed a pushbroom that was just inside the door and unscrewed the handle. I went on into the Captain's office and was handed an ancient gas gun that didn't work, but it made a short club.

"Where are they?" I asked the Captain, who seemed to be paralyzed. (Later I transferred him to an outside assignment.)

"In the kitchen," he finally stammered.

"How many?"

"Not sure," the Captain replied. "I think maybe five."

Deputy Douglas and I met the inmates emerging from the kitchen, and they dropped something on the floor that sounded like knives. Douglas began swinging the broom handle, and I swung my short club. When they recognized us, the inmates immediately tried to give up, so the battle was short lived. However, I still remember the whistle of the broom handle as it whizzed by my head a few times as the give prisoners fell to the floor.

The four inmates had escaped the disciplinary unit by tearing a blanket to strips, catching the night officer,[**] tying him spread-eagled to the bars and securing his keys. After leaving the unit, they went to the main cell houses, took the cell house officer hostage and offered to release the entire block of about 150 prisoners. They got one "taker," released the cell house officer and ran loose throughout the facility until Douglas and I appeared on the scene.

An attempted escape also involved Deputy Douglas and

[**] -The night officer died of a heart attack a short time later.

illustrates how valuable he was as an "inside man." On one weekend, a young man had disappeared without a trace. I was in my office studying the file on the missing man to check relatives and start a search when Deputy Douglas came in and said, "Warden, I think I can find him, but it may create some problems for the institution, and I'd like for you to come with me."

I had great confidence in Douglas so I said, "Lead the way, but let's avoid legal problems if we can."

We went directly to the visiting room where there were about ten visitors. The old visiting room at Buena Vista was a series of booths, six on each side of a small room. Secured on each side of tables in the booths were bench-type seats which were hollow underneath. A mother was sitting in booth #3 visiting her son.

Deputy Douglas walked over to the woman and said, "Lady, would you mind getting out of this booth for a few minutes?"

The old lady was a little frightened, but she complied. Quickly, the Deputy pulled the seat out and turned it over. There was our would-be escapee, *huddled under the seat.* I tried to calm the woman who was close to fainting while Douglas hurried the young man from the visiting room. How Douglas had arrived at the fact that the "rabbit" was in the visiting room and the specific seat he was hiding under attests to a mature "inside man."

My other "best" inside man was Lovell Gentry who had spent his entire career working inside the prison. Appointed a guard at the state penitentiary shortly before the riot of 1929, he had served for more than thirty years in various capacities. He had held positions as guard, Sergeant, Captain and Acting Deputy Warden, finally retiring as Head Captain. In his later years he was visited by such nationally known penal experts as Joe Ragan of Statesville, Illinois, Norton Jamison of South Dakota and Fred Dickson of San Quentin. Although he was invited to their prisons to help train "inside men," he modestly declined.

After a few years at the job, during the early Roy Best era, Lovell began to study the convicts as they came to and went from the prison. He would say, "You have to think like they think!"

From "Cap" Gentry several thousand prisoners received their first talk with anyone in authority at the prison. He said little and seldom smiled, but he was a great listener. He maintained contact with every prisoner and seemed to remember their number, if not their name. He authorized trusty prisoners to do "craft work" and approved every tool allowed. This entailed checking their money accounts and checking to see that everyone in business got a fair shake. He also revoked permits for violations of the terms. He served on disciplinary boards and was considered firm but fair in his judgements. He was a classic example of an inside man whose knowledge of prisoner thinking was vital to the administration's operation of a safe prison. One convict tole me that when he asked for an interview with "Cap" and lined up to talk, he thought Gentry knew what he was going to talk about or ask *before* he got there.

I mentioned that "Cap" seldom smiled, but I recall one day at about 1:00 p.m when I was reading some reports in the prison parole office. "Cap" appeared at the door and said," Pat, I need a little help, and I'd like to show you what I mean."

Following him into the prison main dining room, I could see that lunch time was over and a cleanup crew was working. He led me to the far end of the serving line and pointed out two strange-looking inmates sitting opposite each other at a table. I looked at them and then at "Cap" who grinned and said, "I'd like to see these two paroled."

I knew he was joking, but I looked more closely at the two seated before me. Both inmates were eating with a mountain of food on the table. One inmate was of monstrous size – maybe 400 pounds – so fat that he literally draped over the table, a large wheelchair sitting beside him. He had a half loaf of bread in his hand and was lathering it with butter. The second inmate was a little baby-faced boy who looked to be about twelve years old and weighed about ninety pounds. He was attacking the potatoes, gravy and meat piled high on a military-type steel tray.

Laughing, "Cap" now said, "Warden Tinsley said for us to feed these two, after the "line" had been fed. This is the third loaded tray for the little guy, and the fat one is never full. He's on his fourth loaf of bread and second pound of butter."

I watched for a while, but it was unbelievable what the two ate. With a huge grin, "Cap" said, "Jack* says per meal costs have gone up tremendously since these two have been here! We may need to parole them."**

I said that "Cap" seldom laughed, but when he did, he saw things in perspective!

Captain Clarence Tipton

Someone once said, "The heights great men reach and keep were not obtained by sudden flight; while others slept, they toiled upward through the night." This description certainly fit the Farm Manager at the prison, Captain Clarence Tipton. He lived on the ranch and was on duty *all the time*. He had

Captain Clarence Tipton

little help as he supervised the dairy, the cattle ranch, a slaughter

---

* Jack Cowperthwaite was the prison Business Manager.

** Eventually the fat one was sent to the State Hospital for treatment, and the little one was turned over the prison psychologist for counseling.

house, several hundred acres of farmland, a large orchard, a piggery and a few thousand acres of grazing land. During my time as warden, he had about 300 convicts living in bunkhouses, converted barns, chicken coops and any place that could be made liveable. Never once did I hear him complain. Occasionally, he would ask if I could assign an extra officer to fill in for one who was ill. Cap (as he was often called) was the most innovative of men, sometimes turning the impossible into possible.

The farm and dairy operation was a heavy contributor to self support of the institution, and Cap kept them all running smoothly without modern equipment. He had no tractors for the farm and leveled all of the ground with several spans of mules and draught horses. There were no milking machines for the dairy, which was run by fifty convicts doing the milking by hand. One of the convicts, an old, ex-alcoholic Mexican national doing a long sentence, lived in a converted room in the barn and each day followed a same but necessary routine. His duty was to harness a team of mules, hitch them to a small spring wagon, drive to the hay field, load about ten bales of hay and return to the barn and unload.

Cap was a tough cowboy but very compassionate with the convicts. He told me one time, "Warden, I don't read a lot of these guy's criminal records. I figure that the classification people inside the prison have read them before they were sent out here. I just judge how they perform. If I were to read the records, they would scare me to death." Cap was just a perfect man for the era he served.

Captain Nelson Goerts and Warden Bill Wilson

During my time as Warden, Lieutenant Bill Wilson and Captain Nelson Goerts were my top picks for shift supervisors and middle management. They were strong, mentally and physically. Resourceful and courageous, they were the type you liked to have to back you up – if trouble or violence was faced. Both went on to become leaders at new facilities.

May Gillespie

May was Matron Sergeant, second in command of the women's unit,[*] when I was appointed Warden of the prison in 1965. Shortly thereafter, she was appointed Associate Warden, in charge of the women's unit. She was one of those grand souls that believed thar right and justice would always prevail over injustice and evil. May seemed to me to bridge the gap between people's inhumanity to people, to a teacher of moral values and against the knaves in our society.

She thoroughly understood the multiple problems of women in prison and dealt with the women with daily applications of affection and strength. May referred to the prisoners as her "girls," and she never seemed to give up on mean and tough women. We had some tough and dangerous women, and May was always hopeful that they would change and become lawful citizens.

I consider May Gillespie as one of the outstanding correctional officers with whom I had the pleasure of serving during my career.

_____

* Now the Museum of Colorado Prisons.

Father Justin McKernan (left) and Warden Patterson (right).

Father Justin McKernan

Father Justin was the Catholic Chaplain at the prison, and everyone that I knew (officers, employees and convicts) loved him. He was always available to help in any crisis that might develop. He loved the downtrodden and kept his pastoral door open to all, regardless of their religious preference. He conducted the regular masses, sponsored an in-house magazine, monitored art classes and braille reading classes and, in addition, went out of his way to serve in other capacities. Sometimes he became so involved that he became a "patsy" for a few devious convicts. One incident that I particularly remember was both serious and a little humorous.

I received a note that some convicts were using the father to smuggle pills into the prison. I called the back gate and told the

228

officers there to have the father come to my office as soon as he arrived. Always in good humor, he came into the office smiling and carrying a large picture frame. I asked him to sit down as I intended to discuss the note with him.

On a hunch I looked closer at the frame and asked, "Father, what's the deal on this picture frame?"

"I took it to town for the art group," he explained. "It needed to be repaired."

Taking a screwdriver, I dismantled the frame, and we both looked at a hole drilled in each corner – *containing three pills in each hole*. "I think this is the second time that I had this same frame repaired for the art group, Father Justin explained, thoroughly shocked at what we were seeing. We both chuckled a little, marveling at the ingenuity of the convicts using Father Justin as their drug-toting "mule." Still, I did deliver a short lecture on contraband and told him not to carry anything in or out without telling the Shift Captain or Deputy Warden.

When it came to executions, Father Justin was a master at preparing condemned men for this final act. He was also a great comfort to me during this trying time and in carrying out my other diverse duties. Later, he was replaced as Chaplain, but in my opinion, the job was never filled after Father Justin.

George Levy

George Levy was the prison psychologist. He was a learned professional an also a "character". He never chose the easy cases to work with or evaluate, and he touched the lives of some of the toughest of the criminals.

George could be found in his office in the hospital area of the prison, sitting at a scarred desk topped with a large clay ashtray. In fact, he went through several ashtrays that the convicts molded for him as he would beat on them with the pipe he smoked, and they shattered. Usually he had a convict as an assistant, doing menial tasks and learning something about

Prison Psychologist George Levy

himself. Although George talked tough, this covered a soft heart. Still, if he really got angry, he was extremely noisy, and everyone generally got out of his way.

Part of George's duties was to prepare a psychological evaluation of all prisoners who were scheduled to appear before the Parole Board and the Clemency Advisory Board. He would prepare a very professional report, but he could not resis including a capsulized picture of the inmate. I usually looked for his "one liners" as they were very descriptive, and I loved them as they brought humor to the otherwise gloomy workplace. A couple examples of his clever remarks follow:

- On a public inebriate doing his seventh term: "He goes from bar to bar and then behind bars. He should quit while he's a loser."

- On a habitual criminal, a three-time loser: "We need him like Red China needs metrical."

- On a gang leader of stickups: "He's the type that would start a Klan chapter in Ghana Africa."

- Regarding a prostitute, burglar and ex-model: "She's a sweet kid but has nothing between the earrings and she has spent too much time inside stag- party banquet cakes."

- On a claimed intellectual egghead: "He's a fried egghead, the kind who would take a parachute into a submarine."

- Regarding a former model: "She says she was once a Miss America candidate. It must have been when there were only thirteen states.

- On an elderly prisoner doing a life sentence: "He is a nice old guy but a serious maintenance problem."

When the inmate appeared in person, and I read the capsule, I had to laugh. George tended to describe them perfectly. He was a bright spot that appeared on gray, rock walls, and he was a great help to me during my time at the prison.

Chet Yeo

Chet Yeo was a big, burly touch-minded man who had been appointed as an officer shortly after the 1929 riot. During more than thirty years of service, he became a legend in the prison system. Always in the forefront of any confrontation or violence with prisoners, he was noted for his courage and his fairness and was a born leader among the officers. He had been shot twice and stabbed, nearly lost the sight of one eye in a shootout during the hunt and capture of the 1947 escapees from "Little Siberia."

Many stories were told about Yeo by the convicts, some true and some imagined. I saw an example of his methods when we were called to the west gate bullpen to settle a sit down strike by some thirty convict workers from the "hill gang". Yeo was then the day Head Captain, and he said to me in the presence of the sitting convicts, "Warden, with your permission I'll just kick the asses of this crowd back to their cells."

"You're in charge, Captain," I replied. "You do whatever is necessary, and I'll back you up." The cons took a second look at Captain Yeo, decided that discretion was advisable, got up and headed for their cells.

My second close look at Yeo's methods came one afternoon when a call came that there was a hostage taking up in the school, which was located up a flight of stairs over the kitchen. I climbed the stairs and found Captain Yeo and day shift Captain Ditmore facing two convicts. One was behind the other, holding a broken tobasco sauce bottle to the neck of the first convict. The face of the man holding the hostage convict was contorted with hatred and he yelled, "Cap, don't come any closer or I'll kill this son-of-a-bitch."

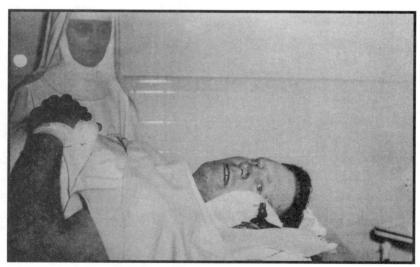

Captain Chet Yeo was wounded during efforts
to capture escaped convicts.

Captain Yeo pulled out his gas gun and calmly said, "Go ahead, Jack. Cut him and then I'll blow your head off. Now turn him loose and you stay alive."

"No go, Cap," the inmate screamed. "I'm going to cut his throat."

Yeo fired the gas gun from about three feet away and both convicts fell to the floor. We all had to duck the tear gas, but I remember how the convicts looked when it all over. Their hair stood straight up in "spikes" and had turned pure white.* As he did other times, Yeo had called the convicts "bluff," and no one was injured.

During his time in corrections, Captain Yeo was admired and respected by everyone who worked for him and also by the prisoners who thought he was always a very fair man.

Earle Meyer and John Dolan

I could not name great professionals with whom I served during my era in correctional services without naming two outstanding Parole Agents – Earle Meyer and John Dolan. Parole in Colorado, as a tool of correctional services, was enacted into the law in 1951, and I was appointed by Governor Dan Thornton as the first Executive Director of the newly created agency.

Both Earle Meyer and John Dolan went to work for the department as their first major work experience – John after graduation from college and Earle after a hitch in the Marine Corps. Both retired from the department after long and distinguished careers. The two were considered honest men who kept their word and "square shooters" by the parolees. I consider them as "number ones" in parole service, and I was always proud to have had a small part in that service.

---

* - Shortly after this incident, the people who made the gas guns marketed a gas spray that took the place of the shotgun-shell blast that loosed the gas from the old guns. The new was just as disabling but was much more

233

George Crouter of the **Denver Post** *(left), Assistant Warden Alex Wilson (middle), and Bill White, Music Director (right).*
Picture taken circa 1968.

Associate Warden Chet Yeo (left), Warden Wayne Patterson (middle), and
Horace Stokes, Captain Colorado Springs Police Department. Stokes and
Patterson has served together as state patrolment in the early 1940s.

Appendix

235

The following paper was presented by Betty Alt on March 14, 2003 in Colorado Springs at a conference of the Society for the Interdisciplinary Study of the Social Sciences. It will give the reader a "tongue in cheek" look at the Colorado State Penitentiary in the 1960s.

THE PRISON AS CITY

During the late summer of 1960, as the morning sun peaked over the eastern horizon and a faint breeze rustled the cottonwood's leathery leaves, the community known as Territorial City began to stir. Inhabitants performed their daily ablutions, cooks prepared breakfast for the early risers, and members of the night shift made their way home for a few hours of shut-eye. As in most communities, it was just the start of another busy day, and with only a few exceptions, Territorial shared the same routines, problems, pleasures and needs of city life anywhere.

However, Territorial was actually a city within a city – the state prison of Colorado – nestled in the foothills of the Rocky Mountains and within the larger town of Cañon City. Although it contained various races, ethnic groups and religious preferences, unlike most cities, Territorial was a community with an extremely high sex ratio. Its population was composed of only forty-four women and approximately 2,256 men. While many of

237

its citizens may have preferred residence in another locale, some spent their entire adult life within its bounds. Others lived there for only a few years while many others moved in and out of the community over their life span. If they ever thought about it, they may have felt fortunate in that they were not required to make a house payment, pay rent, worry about property taxes nor purchase most of the other necessities of daily living.

Another unique feature of Territorial was its resemblance to a mediaeval town. Surrounding it were walls over twenty feet high with towers scattered here and there like sentinels on guard against marauders. The city also contained an irrigation canal, its sluggish water meandering beside manicured lawns and exiting near the east gate.

Territorial's third major distinguishing characteristic was its leadership. It, too, had a mayor or city manager, but he was always addressed as Warden or "boss." Although he had civil servants to help with administrative duties, he had no city council nor group of commissioners who offered advice on Territorial's administrative policies. His authority was absolute, and from time to time he had been given various titles by the community's inhabitants. During his term as warden, Roy Best was known as Czar Best. Wayne K. Patterson in the 1960s and early 1970s had two titles – emperor and beneficent dictator. Other than these few differences, however, Territorial was pretty much like any other city.

Of course, communities cannot exist without a hinterland – an area outside the city boundaries – from which they can obtain a portion of needed products. A large part of Territorial's hinterland was its own farm and a 5,000 acre cattle ranch capable of grazing eighty to one hundred head of cattle. In addition there was a turkey and chicken ranch and a lake populated by large numbers of ducks and geese. This hinterland included a self-contained swinery that could produce three hundred fat hogs per month. Also, there was an abattoir, which usually slaughtered thirty beeves and forty pigs a week, and a smokehouse for curing meat. From these holdings came a portion of the food required by the community's citizens and food for export to outside entities.

As in most cities, six mornings a week the citizens left their living accommodations and went to work to earn money. Some of the individuals labored in an industry known as the "tag plant" which manufactured automobile license plates for Colorado drivers. Another plant constructed highway signs for the Colorado Department of Transportation. Many of Territorial's female inhabitants found work in the city's bakery or its restaurants which provided over 7,400 meals daily. Others worked in the laundry, maintaining the inhabitants' clothing and household linens. Two tailor shops manufactured practically all of the clothing required by residents.

A cannery produced food products which were not only consumed by Territorial's citizens but were sold to schools for their lunch programs. Territorial's dairy of between 300 and 400 cows were milked three times a day, and this product was also consumed by the residents and sent to various charitable and penal institutions. In Warden Roy Best's time, canned goods had been manufactured under the label Best Foods and distributed throughout the country. Like most communities, Territorial had depended occasionally on outside business to bring in additional income. During World War II, the community had contracts to produce uniforms for America's military.

Additional industries and businesses needed to keep a city functioning were available in Territorial. Electrical, carpentry and plumbing shops maintained its administrative, industrial and residential buildings. A number of the inhabitants manned one of Territorial's six busy barber shops or the community canteen which was similar to today's 7- to -11 shopette. Some citizens performed janitorial services, were employed on the farm or ranch or groomed the lawns and flower gardens within and surrounding the city. In fact, a large greenhouse annually provided plants to beautify the landscape near the city's buildings and in its open areas. Formal education for Territorial's residents had become more important in the 1960s, and during the Patterson administration instructors provided classes at the elementary level so that those inhabitants who were illiterate could learn to read and write. Those who had not graduated from high school could obtain a G.E.D. certificate. In addition, a few college level courses were also available. For help with course work, and as a part of leisure activities, a full-service library, plus a law library, was part of the community and was heavily utilized by Territorial's citizens.

Vocational training was also available in several areas and was popular with many. Residents could become proficient in automobile repair and painting, heavy equipment repair and painting, radio and television repair, plus several other areas.

When not at work or in educational pursuits, residents would spend leisure time at the town's movie theater where the most current Hollywood films were screened on the weekends. Football, baseball and basketball teams were organized to play against visitors, and Territorial's teams also journeyed to other cities to compete in numerous tournaments.

Hobbies of one sort or another were extremely popular with residents, and Territorial was known for its "curio shop" which attracted thousands of tourists yearly. In the shop could be found all sorts of art work and crafts – paintings, leather work, stained glass, wood carvings, ceramics, picture frames, etc. Making and selling these items added to the population's income, and the annual gross for the curio shop was approximately $60,000. The town had its own special currency, and a bank for internal exchange was available with a teller window open five days a week to accommodate the citizens' need to add to their savings accounts.

Religious services were held on Sundays for Protestants and Catholics, and religious rites were also conducted for other beliefs as well. Music was provided by a community choir, and often choir members from neighboring towns would visit Territorial to add their voices to the Sunday hymns.

Many other services common to any city were provided to Territorial's citizens. Voluntary firemen hurriedly doused any conflagration, and a large police force preserved order and protected the residents. If violations occurred, and they sometimes did, those individuals disturbing the peace of the city were segregated from the other inhabitants in a short-term segregation area or jail. Usually any disturbance was short-lived, and the normal routine of daily life quickly restored.

Like all communities, Territorial had need of medical services and had available for those who became ill an 80-bed hospital complete with an administrator, a physician/surgeon and citizens who had been trained as surgical assistants and nurses aides. Of course, if the hospital's medical personnel could not accommodate all of its needs, residents could be sent to Cañon City for more specialized attention or hospitalization. For those citizens who suffered from emotional problems or who had been diagnosed as mentally ill, a resident psychologist was available, and Territorial's hospital had a ward set aside for any individuals who had been judged "insane" or continually exhibited violent behavior.

Occasionally citizens met with fatal accidents or simply died of illness or old age. Usually, family members contacted funeral homes who, as in any community, took care of the necessary burial or cremation arrangements. However, for those residents who had no family or were indigent, the city maintained cemetery lots in an area known as Woodpecker Hill.

Territorial is still a thriving community and over the past few decades many cities similar to Territorial have sprung up in states all across America. Today, however, wardens are no longer the sole authorities over these communities, residents are much more concerned with and aware of their civil rights, and populations in many of the new cities are much larger than was the case with Territorial in the 1960s. Still, as in any city, the basic needs of the citizens in these communities have not changed, and, if one were to investigate the newer cities, they would find that many are merely replicas of the old Territorial city.

Colorado State Penitentiary
Cañon City, Colorado

1/10/66

OIC Intake Unit:

Please follow this general outline and dated Rule Book
distribution until further notice.

Wayne K. Patterson, Warden

ORIENTATION LECTURE
TO THE NEW
INCOMING PRISONERS

Good morning! My name is Lt. Marshall, and I am in charge of this housing unit of the prison. It is what we call the "Intake Unit," and you will hear it referred to by the prisoners and sometimes by prison officers as "the fish tank." "Fish" for the first timers and "Suckers" for those who have been here before. In any event, we are here to explain your duties and responsibilities while you serve your sentence. The road you traveled to get here is not our concern at this time.

Now, we didn't send for you; you arrived without our selecting you, maybe not of your free will but the will of the courts. Anyway you are here and this is a penitentiary. Our purpose is not to enter into any debate with anyone as to anything about your sentence. As far as we are concerned, you are here legally, and we are going to do our best to carry out your sentence as ordered by the court. We are going to carry out your sentence in the most humane method possible, but you will have a large part in determining your treatment while you are here.

You can see yourself as tough and create a bit of trouble – you will then discover that we are hired to deal with trouble, ANY KIND of trouble, and the consequences can be harsh and may extend your time here.

Your commitment papers from the courts require that you be committed to the custody of the Warden of this institution until your sentence has expired, you are paroled or otherwise legally released.

You will be required to:

- WORK. I want to emphasize that word.

- Keep yourself and your cell clean.

- Account for your presence here at required times.

Next, I'm going to explain the "count." The count is a very important concern of yours. The cell house officer will tell you when you are to count and where you are to count. As I said, the count is very important to you, and it is very, very important to us. If you are not where you are supposed to be when the count is taken, it causes great consternation among us, and we immediately start to look for you. We become very upset, so you be where you're supposed to be when you are supposed to be there and avoid some serious consequences.

You have been given a number, and this number will be used in all matters that affect you personally while you are here. So, remember it. You will not be paged by your name; you will be paged by your number.

You have been issued prison clothing, and your civilian clothing has been disposed of according to your request. You have been issued prison shoes with a notch cut in the heel. If you are ever caught without the prison shoes or with the heel missing – or you are caught with unauthorized civilian clothing – you will spend time in the disciplinary cells. I can assure you those cells are not very comfortable.

The doctor will examine you shortly, and you are to tell him of any medical problems you may have. The prison is a closed society, and we do not want any diseases brought in from outside. There are more than 2,000 prisoners here and everyone would be exposed. Any legal prescriptions you may have had in your possession have been confiscated. The doctor will re-issue the drugs you need if they are medically necessary.

Anything that is not issued to you or authorized by prison officials is contraband. The law provides additional sentences for smuggling certain items of contraband, and you will be given additional information about this in the rule book which will be issued to you before you leave this unit.

A form will be given to you by the floor officer to be filled out regarding your visitor and correspondent list. You will only be allowed to visit or correspond with those you designate on your list. Visits will only be authorized during your time off from work, except in case of emergencies.

You will be given stamps and envelopes for two letters a week at State expense; any additional materials will be at your expense.

Tooth powder and tobacco will be available at the floor officer's desk. Tooth powder as needed, tobacco issued weekly.

Raise your hand if you are illiterate, that is, if you cannot read or write. If you cannot read or write, say so; and we will assign someone to help you, and they will explain the rules to you.

The Warden sometimes takes guests that nobody else wants, and he asked me to give you one more bit of advice – Do your own time. Don't meddle in the affairs of others.

Do we have questions?

DISCIPLINARY MEASURES
THE 36-DAY DISCIPLINARY PROGRAM*

The prisoner was clothed in coveralls and placed in a cell with no commode or bunk. The isolated cell was equipped only with an oriental ring, which was a round hole in the floor with water running from a source inside the edge of the ring. It was used for both the exiting of body wastes and for drinking purposes. A finger pressed against a water outlet would produce a small fountain for drinking. The ring was used mainly because of the ease of cleaning. Also, prisoners were sometimes "hosed down," requiring considerable drainage.

The cell was equipped with an inside door of steel bars and an outside door that was solid steel. After this door was closed, the cell was completely dark. The cons named it the "hell hole" or "hole" for short.

- The first 10 days consisted of no mattress and a diet of boiled spinach and 3 slices of bread for each meal.

- Then 3 days of full, regular meals and a mattress.

- Then 10 days with no mattress and the bread and spinach diet.

---

* Under Roy Best's administration, the 36-day punishment was in addition to the ride on the "Old Gray Mare." His successor, Harry Tinsley, continued the 36-day treatment, after the whippings were barred by Governor Thornton.

246

- Then 3 days of regular meals and a mattress.
- Finally, 10 days with no mattress and the bread and spinach diet.
- Prisoners were seen by medical personnel daily.

At the end of the 36-day program, the prisoner was removed from the cell and returned to the regular prison population or administrative segregation, depending on the findings of the Disciplinary Board.

During my tenure as Warden, I used the 36-day regimen for most of my term but then limited the disciplinary time as follows:

- 5 days with no mattress and a diet of spinach and bread* for each meal.
- Then 1 day of full, regular meals and a mattress.
- Then 5 days with no mattress and the bread and spinach diet.
- Then 1 day of regular meals and a mattress.
- Then 5 days with no mattress and the bread and spinach diet.
- Finally, 1 day with a mattress and full meals.
- Prisoners were checked daily by medical personnel.

SUMMARY DISCIPLINARY ACTIONS

During the Best era, these disciplinary actions were administered by cell house officers, with the approval of the shift commander.

- **Stringing up:** A handcuffed prisoner was cuffed to the bars of his cell, at a height that prevented his feet from solidly reaching

---

* With the aid of dieticians, I helped develop a loaf of bread containing all the vitamins and minerals necessary to maintain health. It didn't taste very good!

the floor. Punishment could last for an entire 8-hour shift or until "someone" decided that he had been punished enough.

- **Thumb stretching:**[*] If stringing up was not securing the results that the officer felt the convict deserved, the man would be equipped with leather thumb loops and strung up by the thumbs.

- **Standing in the rings:** The rings consisted of a yellow circle about three feet in diameter located near the cell house keeper's station. An errant prisoner was required to stand in this circle for such period of time as the officer deemed necessary to "correct the prisoner's behavior." Reluctance or resistance to standing in the rings could result in a trip to the Old Gray Mare.

There are certain prisoners who fail to understand anything but force. Rules mean nothing, and at times the staff must meet violence with violence. To my way of thinking, only the amount of force needed to secure the safety of the staff and other prisoners should be used – no brutality.

---

[*] Roy Best barred thumb stretching, and Warden Tinsley banished stringing up in the early late 40s, early 50s. Most summary punishments were never recorded.

A RIDE ON THE OLD GRAY MARE

(A word picture of man's inhumanity to man)

I never saw a "spanking," but I have seen the results. During my time as Executive Director of the Colorado State Department of Parole, I had to deal with many inmates who had been spanked and had free access to disciplinary areas. I saw the brutal results of this ritual: buttocks that were purple and looked like chopped liver, gonads the size of a softball, thumbs and ankles swollen to twice their ordinary size. The practice was banned by executive order of Governor Dan Thornton.

I have always been opposed to any type of brutality. Its use leads to more brutality and hatred. I talked to the victims at the time of the spanking and to the same victims several years later. I talked to the officers who participated. I saw the original "Old Gray Mare" as it appeared in storage, and I was privy to its final destination. Finally, I decided that I could comment on the "Mare" and her use. The ritual must be described for the reader to even partially understand:

- The "horse" was an especially sturdy model of a large sawhorse such as a carpenter would use, except it had a step on each side with bracing all around and over the top, making it appear to have a horse's back. The back was covered with blanket material.

249

- The prisoner was stripped of all clothing, except his underwear, and forced to stand on the step facing the horse. A pair of leather cuff-like straps were attached to the steps, and these were fastened to the man's ankles. Then, he was handcuffed with heavy leather cuffs which had a long, leather strap that was threaded through a slot in the step on the other side of the "Mare."

- Two officers would bend the victim over the back of the horse and pull the leather as tight as possible, taking up all of the slack in the cuffs. Now the man would be stretched to the limit, his toes barely touching, his wrists numb from the stretching and his body taut as a violin string. With the aid of a stethoscope, the prison doctor would determine that the man's heart was beating and would signal that the lashing could begin.

- The strap or "bat," used in the spankings was a double thickness of shoe sole leather, three and a half inches wide and about three feet long. The ends of the strap were not sewn, making it similar to a razor strop, and it was long enough to pop and cut the skin. Carved to fit the hands was a handle similar to a baseball bat with a leather thong which tied around the wielder's wrist to keep the bat from slipping out of his hands.* The "party"** was ready to begin.

---

* There were two versions of the bat. The second was more simple – one thickness of leather four inches wide and a shaved-down baseball bat for a handle with four or five brass brads near the end of the leather. Both versions did the same damage to the victim's posterior.

** Some officers referred to the spankings as a "party," and some said, "It's taking this prison back from the convicts."

- Convict John Smalley, who had been spanked several times, told me that the first three or four lashes were not too bad, but after the man's underwear was cut away the skin would get red, then black and blood would spurt from the cuts. John also indicated that the prison doctor sometimes took a turn with the bat, but his strokes were not counted because they were too light.

- Some (officers) said that as many as 125 lashes were bestowed on escapees or prisoners who had assaulted staff. Others said the prisoner was given no set amount, just "what we thought he deserved."

This type of severe punishment was used from the time the penitentiary was built until it was abandoned during Warden Crawford's administration. Then it was brought back by Warden Roy Best as a means of controlling the convicts after the devastating 1929 riot.[*] It was in use at both the prison and men's reformatory until 1951 when Governor Thornton issued his executive order.

---

[*] See *Slaughter in Cell House 3* by Patterson and Alt.

EXECUTION OF LUIS JOSÉ MONGE

Below is the timetable leading up to the execution of Luis Monge.
It is presented here (without editing) from the "scribbled" notes
which I wrote after signing the "death book"
and after interviews with the media.

7:20 p.m. Left home, went to garage and drove to the Warden's Office (Man and woman at Park Gate walking in gusty winds and heavy rain)

7:25 p.m. Went into Warden's Office. Members of the press and official witnesses were in lobby entrance waiting to go in.

7:30 p.m. Came out of office and spoke to Mose Trujillo, Denver Under Sheriff, Captain Stratton and also Don Stimack. Checked with Deputy Warden Fred Wyse regarding readiness for execution and when he was going in. (He indicated he was going in right then.) Mr. Tinsley came in and introduced Mr. Gaddis and also talked for a few minutes. After he left I signed some notes and letters which were on my desk.

7:35 p.m. I went out and asked Mr. Cowperthwaite to have someone pick up my hat and coat at cage of Cell House 3.

7:42 p.m. Phone call from Deputy Wyse at the execution room. We coordinated our watches at 7:42, and I

252

June 2, 1967 — Execution of Luis Jose Monge.

Timetable

7:20 P.M. Left Home went to Garage and drove to the Wardens Office. (There woman at Park Gate waiting in rain) Gusty winds and Heavy rain.

7:25 P.M. Went into Wardens office. members of the Press and official witnesses were in lobby entrance waiting to go in.

7:30 P.M. came out of office spoke to Mose Trujillo Denver Under Sheriff and Captain Stratton also Don Stunach. Checked with Deputy Warden Fred Wyse regarding readiness for execution and when he was going in. (He indicated he was going in right then)

7:30 to Mr. Tinsley came in and Introduced Mr. 7:42 Gaddis and also talked for a few minutes after he left I signed some notes and letters which were on my desk — put our compartmente to have some on file. I went out and added our compartmente to my list and that case file.

7:42 Phone from Deputy Wyse at the Executioner [?]. We coordinated our watches at 7:42 and I told Him to recheck chamber and the Executioner [?] and I also told him to be in the clear so He could make a final check of the Machine, see that Dr. Dwisend was getting Heart, pulse, respiration on the Machine and that I would look for him before operating the lever, I [?]

instructed him to recheck chamber and the execution team, and I also told him to be in the clear so that he could make a final check of the machine to see that Dr. Townsend was getting heart, pulse and respiration on the machine. Told him that I would look for him before operating the lever. I also told him that I would start for the chamber at 7:50 p.m. exactly.

7:43 p.m.   I reread the Execution Warrant from the District Court, the final setting of the date by the State Supreme Court and also rechecked the wording of a Statement of Execution which I had dictated earlier.

7:46 p.m.   I spoke to the switchboard operator Mrs. Prather regarding an injury to her neck which she said had whiplash when her car was hit from behind (She was wearing a neck brace.) I also rechecked her instructions for handling emergency calls.

7:50 p.m.   I put on my hat and raincoat, picked up the envelope with the Death Warrant and started out. The press were crowded in the cage, and I spoke to several that I knew as I passed through the cage – Loy Holman of *The Rocky Mountain News*, Cary Stiff of *The Denver Post*, Doc Little of the *Cañon City Record*. The yard was windy and some rain still falling as I climbed the first steps. I was aware of five or six prisoners with their faces glued to the windows of the main dining room, watching my progress across the yard. The officer on Tower 3 waved and the officer on Tower 8 came out on the catwalk. He waved and I waved back. He called down that he is sure glad the wind has died down. He opens the latch on the C H 3 gate, and I enter the open passageway past the hospital. I am aware of prisoners watching from windows in the hospital. The light on tower 8 flashed on as I went by toward C H 3. A bad gust of wind and rain hit me as I came along the front of C H 3. There was a rising murmur among the prisoners on the lower tier south of C H 3. (Here comes the warden) (Ole Cool Breeze!)

7:53 p.m. The door of C H 3 opened and Associate Warden of Custody Yeo appears. He speaks and I answer. Captain O'Neil, afternoon Shift Captain in raincoat and cap is in the trap and asks if I want to leave my coat and hat. He takes them. I proceed up the ramp to Condemned Row (outside are officers McGinnis and Lt. Atkinson). I step inside and meet Lt. McDaniel.

7:55 p.m. I proceed to Monge's cell (No. 5) which is the next to last. Cell 1 – Garrison is at the rear of his cell (dimly lit). Cell 2 – Young sitting on bed (dimly lit). Cell 4 – Josè Segura lighted up and Joe is standing up. He greets me and I speak to him. (Bell in const* – cell 3.)

7:56 p.m. Monge came toward me from the cell followed by Fr. Justin. I stop him and tell him I must read a statement to him. He says, "Oh, yes! You must read that to me." He and Fr. Justin stood still while I read death warrant statement. We start out of Condemned Row and Lt. Atkinson says we must hold up until the press proceeds on up the ramp to the viewing room at the chamber. Monge is pushing ahead and both Lt. Atkins and I have to lightly restrain him.

7:57 p.m. We proceed up the ramp to the preparation cell. Monge moves at a fast pace, and he and I bump

---

* Constraints

shoulders several times on the ramp. I lightly hold his arm. Fr. Justin follows immediately behind, then Lts. McDaniel and Atkinson. We reach the preparation cell.

Quotes during meeting in Condemned Row to preparation cell.

Monge: *Thank you for your kindness and I hate to do this to you.*

Me: *What do you mean?*

Monge: *I hate to be the one who causes you to have your first execution as I know how you feel about it.*

Me: *It's not your fault; it's the law and I am bound by the law and that's the basis for what's happening here tonight.*

7:58 pm. Monge, Fr. Justin, Lt. McDaniel and I enter the preparation cell.

Monge: *What do I do here? Take off my clothes?*

Me: *Yes and put on those shorts and slippers.*

Monge removes his clothes and puts on the white shorts and the slippers. He sits down in the chair and Dr. Townsend and Dr. Ralston come in with the electrodes which are strapped on his arms and legs. The bands are adjusted and Dr. Townsend squirts a white substance between the skin and the electrodes. Dr. Ralston assists.

Monge: *(To Lt. McDaniel) Lt., thank you for being a good Lt. and man.*

(To the doctor with sly humor) One thing I'd like to know from you doctor. Will that gas in there be bad for my asthma?

Dr. Townsend: *Not for long.*

Me: *Ready?*

Monge: *O.K. Warden.*

Dr. Ralston shakes hands with Monge when he rises from the chair. I take his arm and we enter the chamber room and proceed to the chamber itself.

8:00 p.m. Monge enters the chamber and sits down unassisted. Lt. Wilson and Capt. DeErcole place the black blindfold and strap Monge into the chair. I stand in front of the doorway. Fred Wyse says to me "that's the additional strap over the knees." Capt. DeErcole inspects the straps and pulls the cloth from the pellets. I step into the chamber and asked Monge if he was ready and if he had anything further to say or for me to do and he said:

Monge: *Warden I want to give this to your mother. Will you see that she gets it?*

Me: *Thank you Luis. She will appreciate your thoughtfulness.*

Monge: *Thank you and God bless you.*

Mr. Wyse stepped in when I stepped out and spoke to Monge. Fr. Justin then stepped in and took the rosary from Monge's hand and wrapped it securely around his right wrist. When Fr. Justin stepped out the door was closed and tightened by Capt. DeErcole and Lt. Wilson. Fred said, "Are you O.K., Doc?" and Dr. Townsend said, "O.K." There was a short wait while the acid was released into the vat. Then Lt. Green pulled the safety pin on the lever. I checked both sides of the chamber and the lever dropped.

8:02 p.m. Checked the clock.

Glossary

Big Yard - large section of prison set aside for sports and other recreational activities; consisted of a full size football/baseball field, bleachers on the side and tables at one end where inmates could play cards, etc.

Bueny - the Colorado State Reformatory at Buena Vista was always referred to as "Bueny" by officers and inmates.

Fish - first time prisoner.

Horse-Blanket Dollar - paper money which was somewhat larger than the ordinary bill; some were of different colors.

Intake Unit - prisoner kept in this unit for 30 days before being assigned to regular prison population.

Little Siberia - in cellhouse #6, consisted of 12 cells where prisoners were kept from any contact with other inmates.

Lockdown - If a disturbance arose in the prison, all inmates were locked in their cells. This lockdown could be in effect from several hours to several days.

Mittimus - the commitment paper issued by the court and directed to the warden. Stated that the   prisoner was to be safely kept and at hard labor.

Orientation Lecture - given at some time while prisoner was in the Intake Unit

Pruno (or Raisin Jack) - drink made from prunes, sugar, yeast and water or other combinations of fermented beverages, producing alcohol.

Salle port - open area between two gates or doors to allow one to be closed and locked before the other could be opened.

Screw - prison officer.

Shank - weapon made by prisoner, usually out of an eating utensil, razor blade, toothbrush, file or numerous other items. Prisoners were very resourceful when it came to making a shank.

Trusty - designated by the warden or deputy warden to earn extra good time and have a responsible job.

Woodpecker Hill - back section of the Greenwood Cemetery in Cañon City, specifically set aside for burial of prisoners who either died or had been executed at the prison and whose families had not claimed the bodies.

Writ - written order emanating from the courts.

Zipper - Zip gun, pipe gun – a homemade weapon capable of firing a bullet or shell.